DIAMOND *AT* *YOUR* ROCK BOTTOM

ADVERSITY TO TRIUMPH THROUGH
POST-TRAUMATIC GROWTH

DR. BOLU OLADINI

RIVER GROVE
BOOKS

This book is intended as a reference volume only. It is sold with the understanding that the publisher and author are not engaged in rendering any professional services. The material presented is for informational purposes and intended for self-discovery and to broaden your horizons, but is not intended for treatment. If you suspect that you have a problem that might require professional treatment or advice, you should seek competent help.

Published by River Grove Books
Austin, TX
www.rivergrovebooks.com

Copyright © 2024 Dr. Bolu Oladini

All rights reserved.

Thank you for purchasing an authorized edition of this book and for complying with copyright law. No part of this book may be reproduced, stored in a retrieval system, or transmitted by any means, electronic, mechanical, photocopying, recording, or otherwise, without written permission from the copyright holder.

Distributed by River Grove Books

Design and composition by Greenleaf Book Group
Cover design by Greenleaf Book Group

Publisher's Cataloging-in-Publication data is available.

Paperback ISBN: 978-1-63299-893-4

Hardcover ISBN: 978-1-63299-947-4

eBook ISBN: 978-1-63299-894-1

First Edition

I dedicate this book to my wife, Titi, who saw me at one of my rock-bottom points and still decided to marry me.

ACKNOWLEDGMENTS

I would like to thank Dr. Justin McClinton for his tireless efforts in reviewing and providing feedback on this book. I would like to thank my wife, Titilope Oladini, for having patience with me as I wrote this book. Last, I would like to thank my father, Dr. Lawrence Oladini, for setting a great example for me and inspiring me to be the man that I am today.

CONTENTS

About the Author... ix

Introduction... 1

Part I: Greater Awareness and Utilization of Personal Strengths 5

    Chapter 1: The Obstacle in the Path Becomes the Path 7

    Chapter 2: Let Go of the Illusion of Failure.................... 23

    Chapter 3: Don't Fight Reality 35

    Chapter 4: Rewrite Your Story to Upgrade Your Identity......... 47

Part II: Enhanced Spiritual Development........... 59

    Chapter 5: You Must Go into the Wilderness 61

    Chapter 6: The Answer Is to Question Everything.............. 73

    Chapter 7: Determine Your Values 83

    Chapter 8: How to Stay Resilient on the Journey 95

Part III: Creative Growth 105

    Chapter 9: Sharpen Your Axe for Cutting 107

    Chapter 10: Control Your Breath, Control Your Life 123

    Chapter 11: Two Letters That Will Change Everything.......... 133

    Chapter 12: Building Bridges Gets You Further 145

Part IV: The Identification of New Possibilities and a Purpose in Life 157

    Chapter 13: The Power in Letting Go of Fear.................. 159

    Chapter 14: Listening to Your Inner Voice.................... 171

    Chapter 15: Epilogue: Discover Your Diamond 181

ABOUT THE AUTHOR

 **Dr. Bolu Oladini** is a pharmaceutical industry executive and serial entrepreneur. He is a pharmacist by training with a profitable short-term rental business, a real estate syndication group, and a successful career coaching business. With his background in psychology and a life filled with overcoming personal challenges, Dr. Oladini is passionate about inspiring others to use their adversity as a catalyst for personal transformation. He, his wife, and their two children reside in the suburbs of Chicago, Illinois, where he continues to share his journey and support others in crafting their own stories of success.

INTRODUCTION

What do you do when your whole life falls apart? Many people give up and wallow in self-pity, content to be a perpetual victim or complainer. Although this is a popular option, it's not very productive. Another option is to hope against all odds and somehow have the faith that your life can and will turn around. This path is less traveled but infinitely more rewarding—it is where challenges become the very foundation upon which we build our greatest achievements. Some people give up and succumb to darkness, hopelessness, and nihilism when faced with life's challenges. Other people are able to transmute their negative circumstances into outstanding success and achievement. What makes the difference?

I wrote this book to answer that question. *Diamond at Your Rock Bottom* was written out of my conviction that adversity is not a dead end, but an opportunity. This book is for those trying to navigate the challenges of life, for people who feel stuck in their personal or professional lives, and for anyone who faces adversity but refuses to be defined by it.

Having been through several situations where my life turned upside-down, I know what it takes to create success out of suffering. This book began with the idea to share the lessons I've learned from the significant trials and tribulations that I've faced. These experiences led me to realize that the darkest moments are not merely obstacles to be overcome but are actually opportunities for growth and self-discovery. During a period of deep reflection in April 2020, a time when the world seemed paused in uncertainty, the ideas that became this book were born. The metaphor of uncovering a diamond at your rock bottom perfectly captures the essence of the transformation and growth I experienced over a period of about fourteen years. My vision was clear: to share a message of hope and resilience that could inspire others to see beyond their immediate struggles.

The framework of this book will help you understand. The first step is always self-awareness, which is becoming aware of your behaviors and thought patterns so that you can have the power to change them. The topics, ideas, and questions in Chapters 1, 2, and 3 are designed to help you cultivate self-awareness. The next steps are self-exploration and self-discovery, which we tackle in Chapters 4 and 5. Chapter 6 and Chapter 7 are focused on increasing your self-understanding or self-knowledge. Self-love or self-acceptance is a major theme of this book—and a requirement to proceed to the higher levels. If you discover who you are and you hate yourself, you have no motivation to transform into your diamond. The majority of the rest of the book focuses on self-transformation, before we get to self-actualization in the final three chapters.

Who am I, and why should you listen to me? First, I usually don't like writing about myself in this way, because it feels a little weird, and I also don't define myself with labels or titles. But since you (most likely) haven't met me, I will do my best to describe myself in a few lines. I am a doctor of pharmacy and a pharmaceutical industry executive working (at the time of this writing) at a top-five pharmaceutical company. I am a serial entrepreneur. Currently my partner(s) and I are building a profitable real estate business focused on short- and midterm rentals, another business that does real estate syndication, and a successful career-coaching business. I have an undergraduate background in psychology, and in my past lives, I have been a life coach and podcaster. But most importantly, I have been through the journey I am describing. I have been in seemingly hopeless situations more times than I care to remember, and yet I was able to thrive because of them. The lessons in this book come not just from my formal and informal education, but from what I've experienced firsthand.

There's an entire journey of post-traumatic growth that will take you from rock bottom to creating and uncovering the diamond in your life. The book is structured into four parts, each mirroring the corresponding aspects in the transformative journey of post-traumatic growth: greater awareness and utilization of personal strengths, enhanced spiritual development, creative growth, and the identification of new possibilities and a purpose in life. Each section builds on the previous one, creating a comprehensive roadmap for readers who want to transform their lives.

To those who stand at the crossroads, wondering if the difficult path ahead could possibly lead to anything valuable, let this book be your guide. You are not alone in your journey. With *Diamond at Your Rock Bottom*, you will discover not just how to survive your trials but how to thrive because of them. You hold within you the potential for immense growth and the capacity to unearth the diamond that lies buried at your rock bottom. Let us begin the journey.

PART I

Greater Awareness and Utilization of Personal Strengths

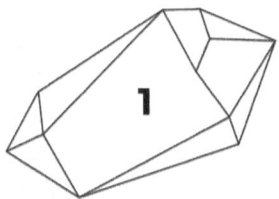

THE OBSTACLE IN THE PATH BECOMES THE PATH

*"Everything negative—pressure, challenges—
is all an opportunity for me to rise."*

—KOBE BRYANT

My world had been shattered.

1. **Situation 1 (2012):** I just failed the class that I needed to get into my pharmacy program. I was overconfident and so sure of myself that I had announced my enrollment into my pharmacy program before I got my final grades. But, like Gandalf in *Lord of the Rings*, organic chemistry said to me: "You shall not pass!" I battled depression for months as I made plans to take the class at a different local college and eventually reapply to pharmacy school. Prior to this, I defined my identity as "the smart kid" who

always did well in school. This definition of my identity was no longer valid. I was in crisis.

2. **Situation 2 (2013):** I just received a mental health diagnosis that usually confines people to a lifetime of medications and doctor's appointments. I have struggled with various mental health challenges over the years. In this particular case, I turned myself into a guinea pig for a clinical trial at my college that was evaluating the side effects of a psychiatric drug. And boy, did it have side effects. When the trial ended and I came off the drug, I had a new onset of psychiatric symptoms that were identical to those of a serious psychiatric condition. And although the symptoms were drug induced and the diagnosis was technically incorrect, that did not change the traumatic nature of my experience. Therapists, psychiatrists, and medications became my new normal, and it took several years before I was able to replace these with natural remedies and lifestyle interventions that enabled me to function at a high level.

3. **Situation 3 (2018):** I just had the woman of my dreams tell me that she doesn't want to be with me. I knew she was the one. I knew she was meant to be my wife and the mother of my children. We had this beautiful connection, and we always brought out the best in each other. I knew I needed to clean up my act in order to be a good husband, but I was still working on it. A

long-distance relationship and communication issues wore her patience thin, as my behavior didn't always match my stated intentions. Eventually, she said she had enough. She was walking away for good. I knew she would forever be the one who got away, so I did everything in my power to get her back. Although I was able to convince her to give me another chance, the prospect of losing the love of your life is always a traumatic experience.

4. **Situation 4 (2018):** I had to change career paths after spending years thinking I would be doing one thing. At this point of pharmacy school, I had been dreaming of a career in the pharmaceutical industry for three and a half years, and I put in a Herculean amount of effort to make it into a reality. This included making the right connections, going to conferences, phone calls, specially selected rotations, targeted extracurricular involvement and leadership, and more; I went the whole nine yards. The most popular path into the industry for pharmacists at this time was what is known as a fellowship. When it came time to apply to and interview for fellowships, I actually did end up getting an offer. The issue, however, was that the salary of the fellowship was low and the cost of living in this particular city was quite high; on top of that, it was a two-year commitment. The real monkey wrench was that I had just

met the woman who would be my wife, and the plan was for her to move from Canada to the US to be with me after we got married. This immigration meant that she would not be able to work for at least a year while we waited for the paperwork to come through. The logistics and timing of this meant that this fellowship offer was a nonstarter if I wanted the marriage to work. I was devastated, as I realized I would have to choose between the two things I wanted the most. I chose the marriage and went with an alternate career path, but I was in anguish for several months as I wondered if I made the right decision. (Spoiler alert: It was most certainly the right decision!)

All four situations had this in common: I had hit rock bottom. Everything I defined myself through and based my identity on was in ruins. My plans were in shambles. I had to question and re-evaluate my life.

Rock-Bottom Opportunity

I am quite familiar with the place known as "rock bottom." No one likes to be there, and people spend their whole lives hoping that they will never get to a point like that. Many people think that their lives are over once they get to a place like this. But I'm here to tell you that there's another side to the story. There is another part of rock bottom that people don't realize:

> **When your life falls apart,
> you get to rearrange the pieces
> how you want them to be.**

There's a diamond waiting for you at rock bottom. The problem is that many of us don't dig deep enough to find it. We're not strong enough to dig for it. We don't have the right tools for the dig. We often lose hope and quit too easily. We don't have the faith that we can find our diamond. Many of us don't believe that we are worthy enough to have something so incredibly valuable inside of us. But the harsh truth is that many of us simply can't withstand the pressure that it takes to form a diamond. The most beautiful diamond can be made from the ugliest piece of coal, but only after it's been under thousands of pounds of pressure.

> **The pressure that will form your
> diamond is your journey of
> self-discovery, personal growth,
> and spiritual awakening after
> reaching rock bottom.**

The diamond is within you, and this book is here to help you discover it.

If you can get past the initial trauma of hitting rock bottom, an opportunity awaits you. Some people run from rock bottom and ignore it, but it is likely that they will soon find themselves at another rock bottom. Life often has a way of repeating situations until you learn the lesson. Every level of your life will demand a better version of you, and the only way to get there is to use the lessons from your rock bottom to level up. An anonymous quote puts it perfectly: "Rock bottom will teach you lessons that the mountaintop never will."

One of the best things about rock bottom is that you can no longer pretend. One of the worst things that so many of us do (and I am guilty of this) is lie to ourselves. You pretend that everything is fine. Even though you hate your job so much that you drink yourself to sleep every night, everything is fine. You've been in the same dead-end relationship for three years, but *now* is when they'll finally change into the person you want them to be, and they will finally want the same things that you want out of life and build a long-term future with you. Everything is fine. But deep down, you have a sneaking suspicion that it's not.

Hitting rock bottom will force you to acknowledge the futility of your self-deceit. All your pretenses will shatter because your dysfunctional behaviors are staring you right in the face. There is no way to get around it. There's nothing like cold hard reality to make you face the facts of your life. Most people aren't motivated to change until the pain of staying the same becomes too much to bear. Dr. Alexander Cortes, a fitness influencer, put it this way on X: "No significant change will take place in your life until you become entirely fed up, disgusted, and unwilling to endure any more of your own bad behaviors. Until that point, you are playing the game of bullshitting yourself." If you never hit your lowest point, all your negative behaviors and delusions will continue to go undetected, eventually creating more problems for you and an even bigger fall down the road.

The motivation to change comes from this simple fact: **All delusion ends once you hit rock bottom.** Therein lies the blessing in disguise. The level of radical honesty that naturally comes from this foundational place is critical for the personal growth needed to create your diamond. That radical honesty will teach you humility. Proverbs 16:18 states that "Pride goes before a fall." Sometimes we need to "fall" in order to keep our pride in check. Too many times, if we never fall, we start to think we're invincible. It's happened to me before. Several times, in fact. You start to think that you're untouchable and you can do no wrong. This level of ego is never healthy, and anyone who has an ego this large is due for a reality check soon.

Unlearning Pride: The Path to Wisdom and Growth

Leo Tolstoy, the famous Russian novelist, once said that "the most difficult subjects can be explained to the most slow-witted man if he has not formed any idea of them already; but the simplest thing cannot be made clear to the most intelligent man if he is firmly persuaded that he knows already." In other words, any concept or idea can be explained to anyone with enough time and effort, as long as that person has an open mind. However, someone who thinks that they have all the answers has no reason to listen to you.

Too much pride and a lack of humility prevent many of us from learning valuable lessons in life. While it would be great if we could always learn these life lessons without the negative experience, this is not what happens many times.

> **When your ego becomes shattered at your rock-bottom point, this is a tremendous opportunity for learning and growth. Many of us are held back in life by our egos.**

According to leadership expert John C. Maxwell, "A wise person learns from his mistakes. A wiser one learns from others' mistakes. But the wisest person of all learns from others' successes." Learning from your own mistakes is the basic level. Only pride will prevent you from going to the next level and learning from the mistakes of others. Your ego will tell you, "I'm better than them," "I'm smarter than them," or "That won't happen to me." You will be completely blind to the negative patterns in your life because of your overinflated sense of importance. And you certainly won't learn from the success of others, because your pride will tell you, "I have to do it my way" or "I can't be like them." When you don't learn from others' successes and mistakes, it's easy to find yourself at rock bottom.

Rebuild the Foundation of Your Life

The truth is this: Hitting rock bottom gives you the opportunity to rebuild the foundation of your life. This is exactly what J.K. Rowling did. When she was writing her first book, she didn't have a job, and she actually received government benefits for a few years, which she later said helped her write the book. When speaking about this time period, she said she was depressed and sought out professional help. In a speech at a Harvard graduation, she said,

> I was set free, because my greatest fear had already been realized, and I was still alive, and I still had a daughter whom I adored, and I had an old typewriter and a big idea. And so rock bottom became the solid foundation on which I rebuilt my life.

She astutely points out that once your life falls apart, there is a freedom that comes with it. If what you fear the most has already happened, things can only get better from that point. The "big idea" was the diamond at her rock bottom, and she was determined to uncover it. You can do the same—you can rebuild your life using your rock bottom as the foundation.

However, you need to first re-evaluate your life. When you were growing up, you unknowingly absorbed beliefs, values, attitudes, perspectives, and a general worldview from the people around you in your environment. These things that you picked up during the formative years of your life may or may not resonate with who you are and who you want to be as an adult. How many aspects of your life have you actually chosen? And how many have you inherited without questioning? The problem is that many people never consciously assess these parts of themselves to make an intentional decision on how they want to live the rest of their lives. Reaching rock bottom is a golden opportunity to re-evaluate and reset these important parts of your life. Don't waste this chance.

From Challenges to Opportunities

Changing your perspective is the first step on the journey to your diamond. There is an opportunity within every obstacle. There is a powerful quote attributed to Roman emperor Marcus Aurelius that exemplifies this idea of perspective:

> Our actions may be impeded . . . but there can be no impeding our intentions or dispositions. Because we can accommodate and adapt . . . The impediment to action advances action. What stands in the way becomes the way.

We can adapt. Where there's a will, there's a way. You must focus on what is in your control. When you focus on what is within your power, you actually increase your power.[1] You can always improve, adapt, and progress.

Adapting and improving requires that we don't define ourselves by the past. If you are constantly replaying the past, you will never be able to move beyond it. And if you are around people who constantly dwell in the past, then it's time to be around some new people. Even if it's your family. Every new moment brings with it new opportunities. Don't be so stuck on what was that you miss out on what could be.

President of High Point University Nido Qubein reminds us that "Your past doesn't determine where you end up. It only determines where you begin." The truth is this: **Your past is only the starting point for your future**. The possibilities are endless. It is only when you continue to identify with the past that you will miss these opportunities. You just have to be able to see things differently. You need a new set of glasses. Allow me to help you shift your vision.

Post-Traumatic Growth: The Path to Your Diamond

In psychology, there is a term called *post-traumatic growth*. Originally researched by Richard Tedeschi and Lawrence Calhoun, this term describes when someone goes through crisis or trauma and experiences growth and development that goes beyond what was there before the trauma.[2] This does not negate the post-traumatic stress that often occurs, and many people with the trauma would prefer that it never happened, but many people can develop great resilience and grow through trauma. In other words, when they reach their rock bottom, they are able to bring out a diamond from it.

Considering that 61 percent of men and 51 percent of women report experiencing at least one traumatic event in their lifetime[3], our overall potential for post-traumatic growth is enormous. Trauma is almost unavoidable in this life; the only question is how we deal with it and what kind of meaning we make of it.

So what makes the difference in those who are able to grow from trauma and those who do not? The research reveals that experiential avoidance—avoiding feared thoughts, feelings, and emotions—actually makes things worse. By not being curious, you shut down your ability to explore, and you cannot generate positive experiences and meaning from the trauma.[4]

Tedeschi and Calhoun have likened the process to an earthquake coming to shake the foundation of your life. Clearly, that does not sound pleasant. Essentially, it's like having your world turned upside down. Not everyone can handle that. But sure enough, they have found that the psychological restructuring that occurs after the trauma or rock bottom "earthquake" is actually necessary for the growth to occur.[5]

> **When your life falls apart, the process of rearranging the pieces together is what creates your post-traumatic growth.**

Honesty, curiosity, and a growth mindset after trauma will lead to the post-traumatic growth on the path to your diamond.

Scott Barry Kaufman reported that people experience post-traumatic growth in seven areas of their lives by growing from adversity:

- Greater appreciation for life
- More appreciation of and building of close relationships
- Increased compassion and altruism
- Greater awareness and utilization of personal strengths
- Enhanced spiritual development
- Creative growth
- The identification of new possibilities and a purpose in life

While all seven outcomes of post-traumatic growth are important, the first three are self-explanatory. I will be focusing on the last four: *(1) greater awareness and utilization of personal strengths, (2) enhanced spiritual development, (3) creative growth, and (4) the identification of new possibilities and a purpose in life.*

Begin the Dig for Your Diamond

If you get to rock bottom, dig deeper within yourself to answer those hard, uncomfortable questions across different areas in your life:

1. **Bad Habits:** Those issues you know you have but don't like to think about. You know, the fact that you drink entirely too much alcohol to ease the loneliness and not think about that one painful situation from the past that still leaves you with regret. Or the fact that you constantly keep yourself busy as a way not to feel the pain that you've been avoiding for years. Or how about the fact that you use food to feel better about yourself? This is definitely not doing your health any favors. Speaking of which, you know how last year, you said that this year was going to be the year that you finally start exercising regularly? What ever happened to that? Why can't you keep any promises to yourself?

2. **Recurring Patterns:** Those same patterns that keep repeating themselves in your relationships. Right when the relationship gets serious, you get scared and run. But somehow you always blame it on the other person. Is there something in your childhood that needs be examined? Do you actually believe that you're worthy of a healthy, fulfilling relationship?

3. **Career Problems:** You're still settling for a career that doesn't suit you. You know that what you're doing right now isn't what you really want to do, but you're too scared. Besides, everyone always told you to pursue this career path. You'd rather play it safe than take any risks. Or at least that's what you tell yourself. But then you see other people with a career that suits them perfectly, and sometimes you get jealous about how happy they are. Something is holding you back. Is it the fear of failure? The fear of the unknown?

4. **Delayed Dreams:** You've been putting off starting that business that you've always wanted to start. "I don't know where to start." "No one would ever buy from me." "I don't have the right connections." All of these excuses you tell yourself. You are continuing to betray yourself. You are delaying your dreams. No one is saying you have to quit your job, but plenty of people start their dream business on the side. Are you afraid of success? Do you have limiting beliefs that are holding you back?

Most people don't like to be alone with their thoughts. We avoid this type of pressure and take the easy way out. We create endless distractions and keep ourselves busy to avoid thinking deeply about these things. But you, on the other hand, must actively seek this pressure. There's no way around it if you want to achieve growth. It's the only way to create and uncover your diamond. As the poet Robert Frost said, "The best way out is always through."

CHAPTER SUMMARY

- When your life falls apart, putting the pieces together is what creates your post-traumatic growth
- The pressure that will form your diamond is your journey of self-discovery, personal growth, and spiritual awakening after reaching rock bottom.
- The way through involves reframing rock bottom as an opportunity to rise and recreate yourself.
- This comes only when you are honest with yourself, you address what has been holding you back.
- Once you start asking yourself the hard questions and take responsibility for your life, you are on the path to your diamond.

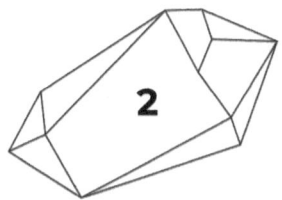

LET GO OF THE ILLUSION OF FAILURE

"There's no such thing as failure. Failure is the reflection of expectation. Without expectation, 'failure' does not exist. Whenever something goes wrong, it is seen as a 'failure' only in comparison to what you had expected it to be. There is no such thing as failure—only lessons. Learn those lessons, move forward, and realize you are better now because of it."

—DR. BOLU OLADINI

There is a Zen story of an old farmer who had been working on his crops for many years. One day his horse ran away. After hearing the news, his neighbors came to visit him. "This is terrible!" they said. The farmer replied, "Maybe, we'll see." The next morning the horse returned and brought with him three other wild horses. "This is wonderful!" his neighbors said. "Maybe, we'll see," said the farmer. The next day his son tried to ride one of the horses. The horse threw him off, and he broke his leg. "What a terrible misfortune!" his neighbors said as they offered their sympathy. "Maybe, we'll see," the farmer replied. The day after, military officials came to the village to draft young men into the army for war. Since his son's leg was broken, they passed him by. The neighbors congratulated the farmer on his good luck. "Maybe, we'll see," said the farmer.

As you can see from this story, what seems to be a terrible failure can actually be a great success. And vice versa. We simply cannot see how things will turn out in the future—what seems to be a "failure" in the moment can actually set you up for success in the future. When you have a more neutral attitude, you can take things as they come and not get swept up in so many emotional dramas. Of course, this is easier said than done.

"Failure" is simply a difference between your expectations and your reality. Without the expectation, failure does not exist. Failure simply means that something did not work. With enough failure, you will eventually learn what works. Take Kobe Bryant, for example. He is one of the best NBA players of all time, but very early in his career, he had a setback he could have viewed as a failure.

In 1997, Kobe Bryant's performance in the Western Conference semifinals against the Utah Jazz became a defining moment in his NBA career, though it initially appeared to be a dismal failure. As an eighteen-year-old rookie, Bryant found himself thrust into a high-pressure situation with veteran

Byron Scott sidelined by an injury. Despite his limited playing time during the season, Bryant took the court with confidence but ended the game with a series of crucial airballs that led to the Lakers' elimination from the playoffs.

During the game, Bryant missed four critical shots, including a potential game-tying three-pointer in overtime. Reflecting on the experience, Bryant identified his fatigue as the primary cause of his missed shots. He recognized that his body, conditioned for a high school season of thirty-five games with ample rest, was not prepared for the rigors of the NBA's eighty-two-game schedule. This self-awareness and analytical approach underscored Bryant's mentality. Instead of dwelling on his poor performance, he viewed it as a diagnostic opportunity to improve his physical conditioning for future seasons.

In an interview for the Basketball Network, Bryant explained his rationale: "The reason why I shot airballs is because my legs aren't there. I got it. Well, next year, they'll be there." This pragmatic mindset allowed him to transform his perceived failure into a learning experience, driving him to tailor his training for the demands of the professional game.

Kobe's reaction to this setback illustrates a powerful lesson in resilience and growth. His willingness to confront his weaknesses and methodically address them exemplified the mindset of a champion. As teammate Shaquille O'Neal noted, Bryant's determination to take those shots, even under immense pressure, was a testament to his desire for greatness. Shaq's encouragement after the game, predicting that Bryant's confidence would one day lead to fear and respect from opponents, proved prophetic as Bryant went on to have a storied career.

From another perspective, Bryant's airballs could have been seen purely as a failure. Critics might have viewed his missed shots as evidence of his unpreparedness or inexperience. Worse yet, he could have used that performance to measure himself, potentially undermining his confidence and reputation. However, Bryant's ability to reframe this moment as a lesson rather than a defeat highlights the transformative power of mindset in turning failures into stepping stones for future success.

"Failure" Is Not What It Seems

Like Kobe Bryant, we need to adapt and learn from each challenge that we face. Once we start telling ourselves a story about this failure and start identifying with it, that is where the loss happens. The idea that you made a mistake will keep you focused on the past, where you can't change anything. But if you learn from every mistake, you won't make those mistakes again in the future. There are only so many mistakes you can make in each area of your life. The problem is that most people do not learn from their experiences. They get lost in the emotions of it all, and then they avoid thinking about it, so they don't feel those negative emotions.

The pain of failure combined with reflection and introspection leads to progress. You can gain a great amount of wisdom when you remove your emotions from past experiences. Most people's problem is that they can't stand the pain, so they skip the reflection, and they miss out on the progress. Very commonly, people end up repeating the same situations over and over again, when, if they just reflected on the situation, they would gain some insight that would move them forward in life. In fact, many of us just repeat the same year over and over again.

When you don't reflect on your life, you can't see what you look like from the outside. So, when someone holds the mirror up to your life, it will seem like an attack. But the truth is that you don't like what's in the mirror. If you cultivate self-awareness by reflecting on your life regularly, your failures are only lessons that will build the foundation for your success.

Human beings are the only creatures on this planet that have been blessed with the gift of metacognition. Metacognition is defined as "thinking about your thinking" or being aware of your own thought processes. In truth, other than our ability to vocalize, metacognition is really the only thing that separates us from other animals. Although this may be up for philosophical debate, I believe metacognition is what truly gives us consciousness. Yet so many of us are unaware of our own thoughts. It is only through examining your failures and learning from them that you can progress in life.

One way to think about failure is "Never make the same mistake twice." When you focus on what you have learned to apply it in the future, that is the real value. The real question is what you can learn from each mistake. You have actually gained the knowledge of what does not work. Once you continue amassing this knowledge, you will eventually find out what works.

There Are No Mistakes in Life, Only Lessons

Learn, learn, and learn some more. There are no mistakes in life—only lessons. Change your mindset to a growth mindset—either you win, or you learn. And learning is still winning, so you're in a win–win situation if you have the right perspective.

Failure is not final; failure is feedback.

When you embrace lifelong learning and become a student of life, you will realize that everyone and every situation has something to teach you. Yes, including your "failures." Especially your failures.

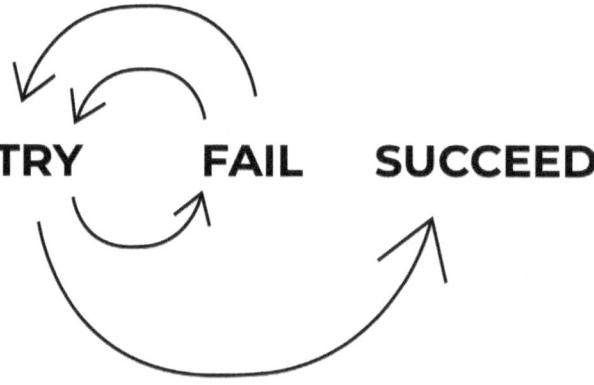

2.1 *Try Fail Succeed*

Most people learn more from failure than success. People get too caught up in celebrating success, and then they fool themselves into thinking that they can't fail. Failure is often the best teacher. Experiencing too much success too early on can be a trap. This is because people tend to attribute success largely to their own talents and efforts and usually downplay factors such as luck, timing, and other external factors they do not have control over. In psychology, this is called the *fundamental attribution error*.[1]

If you always succeeded at everything you did the first time, eventually you would think you were infallible and could do no wrong. The truth is that early success breeds arrogance. Early failure, on the other hand, increases wisdom, especially if you have the right perspective. Don't become defeated by success.

Kodak's Moment Comes to an End

Kodak is an example of a company that was defeated by their own success. The company was founded in 1888 by George Eastman and quickly became a leader in the photography industry. The company was known for its innovative products and technologies, including the first roll film camera in 1888 and the first color film in 1935. CEO George Fisher led the company from 1993 to 2000 and was known for his focus on traditional film and print technologies. Despite pressure from employees and shareholders to invest more heavily in digital technology, Fisher resisted change and maintained Kodak's focus on film.

Dhananjay Mittal discussed this in a Medium.com article. As digital cameras began to gain popularity in the late 1990s and early 2000s, Kodak's dominance in the market began to wane. Despite being one of the first companies to develop digital cameras, Kodak failed to fully embrace the technology due to their reliance on film. Kodak's unwillingness to fully embrace digital technology ultimately cost them their market share. In 2012, the company filed for bankruptcy, citing the rise of digital photography and the decline of traditional film as the main reasons for their financial struggles. While Kodak was once a leader in the photography industry, their past success ultimately became their greatest enemy. Their reliance on film and print technology prevented them from adapting to changing consumer preferences and ultimately led to their downfall. Recent history is littered with examples of companies whose success blinded them to future failure. Think about Blockbuster, which is now an almost forgotten name in the rental industry.

Growth Mindset Affects Potential

Many people who have a fixed mindset, like Kodak's George Fisher, really struggle dealing with failure. The idea of a fixed mindset, popularized by author Carol Dweck, means that you believe people's traits and skills are fixed—it's about validating yourself and proving that you're smart, over and over again. People with a growth mindset, by contrast, believe that skills can be cultivated with effort. They thrive on challenges and focus on learning.

According to Dweck, "One key difference is that the fixed mindset focuses on how you are being perceived by others, whereas the growth mindset is focused on internal improvement." [2] As a result, having a fixed mindset can increase people's fear of failure because they are more likely to believe that failure reflects their innate abilities. It can also lead to a lack of motivation to improve, since they believe their abilities are fixed and can't be changed. A growth mindset, however, makes people more likely to embrace challenges; this is because any "failure" would be a reflection of their effort and not their natural ability. Of course you can always change your effort, whereas you can't really change your natural ability in any particular area.

The Growth Mindset in Business

The fixed and growth mindsets certainly apply in business. Take Domino's Pizza, for example. Domino's Pizza, founded in 1960, quickly became synonymous with quick delivery and convenient service. Their promise of delivering pizza within thirty minutes was a hit in our fast-paced society. By the 1990s, Domino's had become a behemoth in the pizza delivery industry, an accomplishment that many would label as the pinnacle of success. However, by the mid-2000s, Domino's faced a harsh reality. Customer satisfaction was at an all-time low. By 2009, Domino's faced critical customer feedback, with complaints about the quality of its pizza being likened to "cardboard" and "ketchup."[3] A company with fixed-mindset leadership would have seen this as a failure, and perhaps it would have led to layoffs or filing bankruptcy.

However, the CEO of Domino's had a growth mindset. Instead of denying the problem or merely making superficial changes, Domino's took a bold step. Under the leadership of J. Patrick Doyle, Domino's embarked on an ambitious and brutally honest marketing campaign in 2009, openly acknowledging its past mistakes and committing to significant changes in its product. This marked the start of a comprehensive overhaul, in which new recipes were tested, ingredients were upgraded, and customer feedback was actively sought and incorporated. These are all the hallmarks of a growth mindset.

The results of this transformation were staggering. Domino's experienced a substantial increase in customer satisfaction and financial performance. The company's approach to innovation extended beyond its product to embrace cutting-edge technology, setting new industry standards in the process. By 2019, Domino's had achieved an annual revenue of $14 billion and showed a consistent increase in same-store sales.

Domino's story illustrates the danger of complacency, the importance of acknowledging failures, and the power of a growth mindset. There is always another mountain to climb, another challenge to overcome. The company was willing to acknowledge its shortcomings, learn from customers, innovate relentlessly, and adapt to a changing market landscape. True success is not a destination but a journey marked by continuous growth and adaptation.

Failure Does Not Exist

You have to shift your perspective from a fixed mindset of winning and losing, from the limited binary of success and failure to a growth mindset that prioritizes learning above all else. When evaluating your experiences, ask yourself, "What did I learn from this situation?" "What did this situation teach me?" and "How did I grow from this experience?" That is the true measure of success.

At the end of the day, failure does not exist. The only real "failure" is not learning from your experiences. The only "failure" is to stop trying. If you don't succeed on Monday, it's only a failure if you don't learn anything and don't try again on Tuesday. And Wednesday.

CHAPTER SUMMARY

- One of the first steps on the journey to your diamond is changing your relationship with "failure."
- Reaching rock bottom is not a failure; it's a learning opportunity.
- You have the opportunity of a lifetime: you have the chance to embark on the journey to discover your diamond. Don't waste it.

- Develop a growth mindset, reflect on your life to learn the lessons, and realize that success is a continuous journey—meaning failure does not truly exist.
- Once you have let go of the illusion of failure, you will be ready for the next step of the journey.

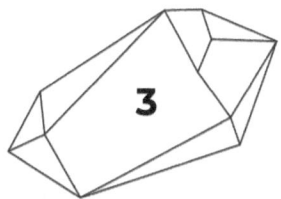

DON'T FIGHT REALITY

"Whatever the present moment contains, accept it as if you had chosen it. Always work with it, not against it. Always say 'yes' to the present moment. What could be more futile than to create inner resistance to what already is? What could be more insane than to oppose life itself, which is now and always now? Surrender to what is. Say 'yes' to life—and see how life suddenly starts working for you rather than against you."

—ECKHART TOLLE, *A NEW EARTH*

The word "should" is a very dangerous word. By its very nature, "should" is at odds with reality. When you say a situation *should* be different than it is, you are not accepting the present moment for what it is. "Should" is working against the present moment instead of working with it. "I should go to the gym right now." "I should be working on this assignment right now." "I should go out and meet more people." When you say these phrases to yourself, how does it make you feel? Does it instantly motivate you to take action? Chances are, probably not. When you use the word "should" on yourself, you automatically create feelings of guilt and shame. Do these negative emotions actually get you any closer to your goals? Most likely not. Whenever you "should" yourself, this implies that there is a gap between what you know you must do and what you are actually doing.

This lack of alignment between your thoughts, feelings, and actions is in fact a warning light, if you pay attention closely. Perhaps you need to listen to your body. Maybe you are forcing yourself to work when you really need to rest. Maybe you are trying to be productive when you need to have some fun instead. Maybe you are holding on to someone else's expectations of how they think you need to live your life. Or maybe you are pursuing a course of action that made sense in the past but no longer aligns with who you are at this present moment and your true life's purpose. In short, perhaps you are not listening to your own intuition and inner voice.

When you have this lack of alignment internally, it's quite possible that you are forcing yourself to do something that you truly have no desire to do. If it's a simple matter of preference, then choose something else, by all means. For example, if your parents want you to major in biology and go to medical school, you can have the courage to choose another major and another career path.

However, if you have no desire to do something that will clearly and definitively benefit your life and the alternative will not, you need to ask yourself further questions. If you have no desire to eat healthy and exercise, for example, then maybe you lack the self-discipline to follow a meal plan and an exercise regimen. Maybe you've been conditioned to look to food as comfort and stress relief instead of as fuel and nourishment. If you have no desire to end an unhealthy, toxic relationship, for example, then perhaps you need to closely examine your childhood relationships in therapy. Maybe you don't feel worthy of a healthy relationship and you've normalized toxic behaviors. Regardless of the situation, any time you are forcing yourself to do something you do not want to, you need to examine the situation more closely.

Accept Reality

When you use the word "should" in reference to the outside world, it can be even more counterproductive. When you say the world "should" be a certain way, it carries with it self-righteousness, arrogance, and hubris—that *you* are the one who determines how life must unfold. It carries this assumption that you are in control of everything. And that, of course, could not be further from the truth. In order to find your diamond, you must accept the fact that there are many things that you have no control over.

You need to embrace reality in the moment, without resistance or denial, regardless of the pain it may bring. Recognize what is beyond your control, and choose to respond to it effectively and without unnecessary struggle. For example, consider someone who has unexpectedly lost their job. Practicing radical acceptance would mean acknowledging the situation without judgment, recognizing it as a part of life's natural ups and downs, and moving forward without ruminating in anger or self-pity. It allows the individual to focus on actionable steps, such as updating a resume or networking, rather than getting stuck in a loop of what could have been or overanalyzing why it happened.

Acceptance Requires Emotional Maturity

Accepting reality requires a certain level of emotional maturity. It takes maturity to realize that things can't always be the way that you want. Yet so often many of us are stuck at that childish level of emotional maturity where we think or say things like "That's not fair!" or "I deserve better!" or "It shouldn't be that way!" The truth that all of us above a certain age (or maturity level) know is that life isn't fair and no one really deserves anything. It's quite sad to see many grown men and women these days throwing a temper tantrum and generally having a fit when something doesn't go their way. It's not entirely their fault, however, because many people coming of age today have been lied to throughout their childhood. Being told that you deserve special treatment, participation trophies, and all the best things in life for simply existing is not a good recipe for dealing with reality.

> **Too often people try to adapt reality to fit their emotions, instead of adapting their emotions to fit reality.**

The harsh truth is that reality does not care about your emotions. Instead of "should," you can say, "It would be better if." This way, you focus on the future that you can change instead of the past that you cannot change. This way, you also acknowledge that you cannot always dictate how life goes. Instead of focusing on "should," focus on what you *want* to do and why. "Why do I not *want* to do what is best for me? Is that really what is best for me? Is there something I need to be doing instead?" This line of thinking will be much more productive. For example, "I should go to the gym" becomes "It would be better if I went to the gym." From there, you can ask yourself, "Why do I not want to go to the gym? Maybe I need to make it more enjoyable. Am I doing the wrong kind of exercise? Maybe I need to listen to different music." This way, you can actually get to the root of the issue instead of just "should-ing" yourself to death and feeling guilty and ashamed.

Deal with Things as They Are

To find the diamond waiting at your rock bottom, you must delete the word "*should*" from your vocabulary. "*Should*" will keep you stuck on what has happened to you, and it will keep you forever a victim. Any time you tell yourself that something "should" be a certain way, you are creating inner tension in your mind. It expresses a fundamental dissatisfaction with some part of life. It removes all gratitude from your life by default, because you cannot be grateful when you think that something should be different from what it is or from what it was.

When you are in denial, this nonacceptance of reality will keep you at odds with the world and prevent you from achieving your full potential. How can you have inner peace if you are not at peace with reality? How can you have peace inside yourself if you are not at peace with the outside environment? By trying to fight reality, you will put yourself in a battle that you can never win. Don't fight reality. Embrace it and deal with it. You must deal with the world as it is, not as you wish it would be.

Carl Jung, the father of analytical psychology, points out that "we cannot change anything until we accept it. Condemnation does not liberate, it oppresses." If you never acknowledge the reality of the situation, you can never deal with it properly. To be in denial is to abdicate your power to transform your circumstances. As it's commonly said in addiction recovery programs, "The first step to getting help is admitting you have a problem." You can't help someone who doesn't realize they need help, just as you can't improve your life if you don't accept the basic truths about your life.

Keep an Open Mind

A major step toward being at peace with reality is being open-minded. But there's a major challenge to keeping an open mind. Usually, it's our egos that close off our minds to other possibilities. At a certain point, you think you know it all, and then no one can tell you anything. I've fallen victim to having an oversized ego as well. However, I'm not the only one.

Before the 2020–2021 NBA season, the Los Angeles Lakers traded for point guard Dennis Schroeder. He was coming off one of his best seasons, and the Lakers were looking for a third star player to pair with Anthony Davis and Lebron James. However, this was a contract year for Schroeder, which meant he would become a free agent at the end of the season without a new contract. This also meant that he could walk away for nothing after the Lakers traded assets to get him. When he started off the season strong and was putting up great numbers, the Lakers wanted to keep him, so they offered him a four-year, $84 million contract extension.

He had gone from a being a bench player on his previous teams to demanding to be the Lakers' starting point guard, so you would think that would be enough. He actually got the starting job, but he reportedly wanted a $100 million contract! So Schroeder declined the $84 million contract extension offer. He bet on himself. However, his play fell apart in the playoffs, and he actually registered a ZERO-point game in the Lakers' first round loss to the Phoenix Suns. Zero points! During free agency the next year, nobody would pay him the money he wanted, so he signed with the Celtics for one year, for $5.9 million. It's safe to say Dennis Schroeder's ego was too big for his own good—it cost him $78 million, after all.

What is the ego? The ego is the part of yourself that has the constant need to see itself in a positive way.[1] It's the part of you that never wants to admit that you're wrong. It never wants to apologize.

> **Your ego is more interested in self-preservation than the truth. Your ego would rather make sure you look good than make sure you learn something new. Your ego prefers being right to finding the truth.**

Beginner's Mindset

Author Shunryu Suzuki makes an important distinction in his book *Zen Mind, Beginner's Mind*: "In the beginner's mind there are many possibilities. In the expert's mind there are few."[2] The beginner usually has little to no ego, but the expert typically has an enormous ego. For most people, their ego increases with their knowledge, success, and achievements. This is a very common trap that people fall into. How do you avoid this trap?

Maintain a beginner's mindset. One facet of such a mindset is radical open-mindedness.

Ray Dalio perfectly encapsulates the beginner's mindset when discussing open-mindedness as quoted in a Farnam Street article:

> True open-mindedness is an entirely different mindset. It is a process of being intensely worried about being wrong and asking questions instead of defending a position. It demands that you get over your ego-driven desire to have whatever answer you happen to have in your head be right. Instead, you need to actively question all of your opinions and seek out the reasoning behind alternative points of view.[3]

A beginner's mindset requires that your joy of learning is stronger than your need to be right. This will help you to remain humble, and it turns you into a "learn-it-all" instead of a "know-it-all." When we approach things with a beginner's mind, we remain curious and we acknowledge that we don't know everything and that there's always more to learn. This perspective will prevent you from developing an inflated ego. Another benefit of this mentality is that you are more receptive to feedback and other people's ideas.

Many of us are afraid of being a beginner. We're scared of not having all the answers. We have a false sense of security that comes from being perceived as an expert. Effectively, our knowledge zone becomes our comfort zone. This holds us back from growing and expanding in additional areas of our life. Some of us are only comfortable as long as we're in control, and the way we exhibit this control is through our knowledge.

You need to get back to that state of mind where you only want to learn, and there is no ego to get in the way. This is a state where you are open to *all* possibilities, where you are ready to doubt any of your beliefs if given enough evidence. Can you accept new beliefs and opinions, even when they fly in the face of everything you've thought for years?

Learn It All

The difference between being a learn-it-all and being a know-it-all is the difference between the joy of curiosity and the fear of the ego. When you are driven by curiosity, your goal is exploration. You are not trying to confine reality to a predetermined destination or path. You are open to possibilities. You are much more likely to think creatively and come up with innovative solutions to problems.

When you are a know-it-all, by contrast, reality *must* fit into your predetermined ideas and constructs. When it does not, one of two things typically happen. Either you deny reality and come up with a false or nonsensical reason why reality does not match your preconceived notions, or you have an existential crisis, since your identity as a know-it-all has been shattered. Something important to note is that people usually don't think of themselves as know-it-alls, but the people around them always notice.

There's a very simple test to figure out whether you are a know-it-all or a learn-it-all: When you are confronted with information that contradicts your previous beliefs, do you get defensive and dismissive, or do you get curious and try to find out more information? The former would make you a know-it-all, and the latter means you are a learn-it-all and have a beginner's mindset.

The key is to stop identifying with your beliefs and opinions. You are not your beliefs. Your opinions are not a part of your identity. You need to have a certain level of curiosity about life. Assume you can learn something from everyone. Once you do this, an attack on your beliefs is no longer a personal attack on yourself. If someone challenges your opinions, you won't feel that they are challenging who you are as a person. Changing your mind is not a sign of weakness; it's a sign of strength.

CHAPTER SUMMARY

- Embrace reality as it is; not as you wish it would be
- Acceptance requires emotional maturity—this means you need to adapt your emotions to fit reality, instead of trying to adapt reality to fit your emotions

- Keeping an open mind requires that you remove your ego attachment to always being right; you want to be a learn-it-all and not a know-it-all
- When you stop identifying with your beliefs, you can approach things with curiosity and realize that changing your mind is a sign of strength, not weakness

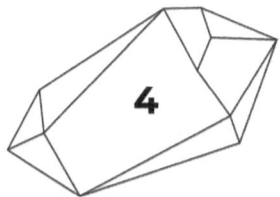

REWRITE YOUR STORY TO UPGRADE YOUR IDENTITY

"The only thing that's keeping you from getting what you want is the story you keep telling yourself."

—TONY ROBBINS

Dwayne Johnson, also known as The Rock, really wanted to be an NFL player. He played high school football and went to the University of Miami on an athletic scholarship to play football, one of the top college football programs in the country. He tried his hardest, but his dream of being in the NFL never came true. He went undrafted in the 1995 NFL draft, then signed with the Calgary Stampeders in the Canadian Football League but was cut in his first season. Later that year, he was signed by the Miami Dolphins and played for their practice squad for several months before being released.

Imagine if he had gotten his wish. The average NFL career is a little over three years, so he would have played for a few seasons, made a few million dollars, and put himself at very high risk for developing the brain disease known as chronic traumatic encephalopathy (CTE). **Instead, he reimagined his identity and reinvented himself as professional wrestler and eventually an actor.** Amazing things can happen if you let go of your current identity to make room for something greater. It's only, as Lao Tzu said, "When I let go of what I am, I become what I might be." Dwayne Johnson is one of the most successful actors in Hollywood, so it's a good thing he was able to let go of his identity as a football player. He's gone on record about his NFL journey and, in an Instagram video, said, "You gotta have faith that the one thing you wanted to happen oftentimes is the best thing that never happened."

Have faith. It's the only way you can get through the uncertainty of letting go of who you are. Have faith in yourself. Have faith that something better is coming. Have faith that you can make it through. Have faith that you are being guided to where you belong. Have faith that it will all make sense in the end. Life happens to us looking forward, but things only make sense looking back. You don't know what's waiting for you on the other side of your current identity.

You cannot find the diamond at your rock bottom without shifting your identity. The same way coal must change its identity to become a diamond, you must change your identity from your coal to become your diamond. The coal and the diamond are fundamentally the same on the inside. They are both made of the same carbon, but the diamond has undergone thousands of pounds of pressure to become something better, something greater, something more valuable.

Change requires maintaining a flexible identity. If you identify too strongly as one inflexible thing, then you cannot upgrade your identity and reach your true potential. You must undergo a refinement process to shift your coal identity to your diamond identity.

Our Stories Become Our Identity

The way you do this is through your words. Your words create your beliefs, and your beliefs create your identity. Your words have power. Your words create stories about yourself, and the stories you tell yourself determine your identity. So, in essence, the things that you tell yourself shape your reality. What you believe about yourself and the world creates a self-fulling prophecy.

The more you tell yourself the same stories, the more those stories become part of who you are. What you say about yourself greatly affects your identity. If you say, "I'm not good at math" or "I'm terrible with remembering names," you are making that into part of your identity, and you won't be able to move beyond it.

Your brain constantly searches for evidence of what you believe. When you have deeply held beliefs, conscious or unconscious, your mind will *not* search for evidence to the contrary. In fact, most times it will ignore any information that opposes your beliefs. In psychology, this is called *confirmation bias*. It means that you are more likely to seek out information that confirms what you already believe and, conversely, ignore any information that contradicts those beliefs.

So, if you believe that you are a loser, your mind will constantly search for evidence that you are a loser. If you believe that nothing good ever happens to you, your mind will ignore the good things in your life and focus on and magnify the bad things. If you believe that there are no good men or good women out there when it comes to dating, then this is exactly what you will experience. Your subconscious mind will overlook the good people, and you will focus on the people who are bad relationship prospects, because that is where your attention is. The good people won't be attracted to you, and you won't be attracted to them, because your belief system does not acknowledge that these people exist. Therefore, they must be "too good to be true" or they must be hiding something. Because of this, you need to be careful how you talk to yourself so you don't subconsciously create any limiting beliefs about yourself or the world.

A Primer on the Subconscious Mind

But what is your subconscious mind? Dr. Joseph Murphy explains this in his book *The Power of Your Subconscious Mind*. He likens the conscious mind to the captain of a steam-powered ship, while the subconscious mind is like the men operating the engine room. The captain directs the ship on where to go, but the men in the engine room operate the machinery that actually drives the ship. The captain (conscious mind) gives the orders to the men in the engine room (unconscious mind). They have no idea where they are going and simply follow orders. They would drive the ship onto the rocks if the captain gave bad orders. The men in the engine room do not talk back; they simply obey the captain because he is in charge.[1]

Your subconscious mind will always believe what your conscious mind tells it, no matter how incorrect or damaging it may be. Your subconscious mind cannot reason or argue with your conscious mind and cannot take a joke. It literally takes everything you say at face value. It's critical to make sure you are giving the correct orders to your subconscious mind. Therefore, you need to eliminate any false or limiting beliefs that you have about yourself.

You have to be careful how you talk to yourself because your subconscious mind is listening. Proverbs 18:21 (King James Version) states that "Death and life are in the power of the tongue." If you say, "I'll never lose weight," your subconscious mind will see to it that you continue to make bad food choices that will undermine your health and keep you overweight. This is the same idea that people refer to when they talk about a "self-fulfilling prophecy" or "speaking something into existence."

Change Your Inner Story

Talking ourselves into existence means that changing your own inner narrative is the key to changing your identity. Don't blindly listen to the narratives that you or others have created about yourself. You need to question and evaluate all of these conscious and unconscious stories about yourself that are floating around in your head and reject the stories that no longer serve you. Are you really what your family, your friends, your colleagues, or society has labeled you as? Or are you something more?

Don't be afraid of your power. Don't be afraid of your capabilities. Don't be afraid of leaving other people behind or outshining them. You are not doing the world any favors by limiting yourself.

You need to rewrite your own story. You are the author, the actor, and the director in the movie of your life. If you haven't acknowledged this power until now, it's never too late. Don't let someone else write your story. Even if you don't like the first few chapters of your story, turn the page and start a new chapter.

If we are unwilling to write our own story, the world will do it for us. As Carl Jung stated, "The world will ask you who you are, and if you don't know, the world will tell you." Human beings have relied on labels and stereotypes for centuries. This makes sense from an evolutionary perspective—our brains always want to take shortcuts so we can conserve mental energy. However, this becomes a problem when we start to buy into these labels and allow them to define us. It is up to you to define yourself and make sure that your inner narrative is empowering and leads you to become your highest self.

Very frequently, our identities are based on different roles we had growing up, whether in school, in our families, or with our friends. The stories we tell ourselves usually come from these roles. But the problem is that these stories do not change as our roles change. This role change occurs, but often our identities do not change with them. Your identity needs to be shaped by your true character and not just the roles you have had and outgrown at different points of your life.

Many of us still stick to identities that no longer serve us. If you cannot let go of your identity as the star quarterback on your high school football team, you'll have a hard time adjusting to working in the real world, where most people have to start at the bottom and work their way up. If you can't let go of your identity as the prettiest girl in college who all the guys want to date, you may find it hard to adjust if you find yourself single ten years later and fifty pounds heavier. If your entire identity is based on your job, you may find yourself depressed if you get laid off instead of using the opportunity to do a career pivot and/or start your own business.

Break Out of Your Comfort Zone

The main problem that holds many people back from changing their identity and their own internal narrative is that they are scared of change. The reason that they are afraid of the unfamiliar is that they prefer the certainty of their current beliefs, even if they are limiting. But even the best of us, those who find the diamond at our rock bottom, are comfortable being uncomfortable. Your comfort zone is where your dreams die. *All growth occurs outside of your comfort zone.* You can grow, or you can be comfortable, but you can't do both. You will never create your diamond in your comfort zone. You must prioritize growth, and growth requires change.

In your comfort zone, you feel safe and in control (see Figure 4.1). Most people get to their comfort zone and stay there their whole lives. It is low risk, but it is also low reward. Once you leave your comfort zone, you move to the fear zone because fear is the natural response to leaving our comfort zone. In this area, you are very much affected by others' opinions, and you readily find excuses. This is also usually accompanied by low self-confidence. Most people don't make it past the fear zone. They feel the fear and retreat to their comfort zone.

If you can be one of the few who makes it out of the fear zone, you will reach the learning zone. It is here that you face challenges and solve problems. But most importantly, you acquire new skills and actually extend your comfort zone. Learning is the critical step here. Last but not least, we have the growth zone. It is here that you set new goals, conquer objectives, and eventually live your dreams and find your purpose. This is easier said than done, and it is a continual journey. If you want to create and uncover your diamond, you need to spend most of your time in the growth zone. This is where your diamond is hidden.

THE COMFORT ZONE

Diagram showing four concentric zones:

- **COMFORT ZONE** (innermost): Safe and in control; Low risk, Low reward
- **FEAR ZONE**: Low self-confidence; Find excuses; Affected by others' opinions
- **DIGGING ZONE**: Face Challenges; Problem-solve; Acquire new skills; Conquer objectives
- **DIAMOND ZONE** (outermost): Find purpose; Live dreams; Set new goals — This is where you want to spend most of your time

Extended comfort zone encompasses the Fear and Digging zones.

4.1 *The Comfort Zone*

Embrace Uncertainty

To create your diamond and shift your identity, you must embrace uncertainty. You must become comfortable with the unknown. As you question the stories that have shaped your identity, you will eventually get to the point where you question your current identity. If you get to the point where you think to yourself, *I don't know who I am anymore*, then it means that you are making progress. As crazy as it might sound, if you get to the point where you have an "identity crisis," that is actually a good thing.

> **The best part about not knowing who you are, is that you can be anyone.**

The fact is that you must consciously decide who you want to become. The power in not knowing who you are is that you can then make the *decision* to become your highest self. You can make the decision to create a diamond from your coal. The truth is that becoming the best version of yourself will require you to continuously update your beliefs and positively change your identity. The negative connotation that is usually associated with an identity crisis comes from the underlying belief that we are supposed to know who we are at all times. When you can accept the uncertainty of not knowing who you are for a time, you can allow a deeper level of self-knowledge to emerge.

This apparent paradox presents a problem because most of us have an incessant need to be able to know and explain everything in our lives. According to *Cambridge Dictionary*, a paradox is defined as "a statement or situation that may be true but seems impossible or difficult to understand because it contains two opposite facts or characteristics." There is a special power in the paradox, however. Psychologist Carl Jung argued that "only the paradox comes anywhere near to comprehending the fullness of life."[2] As much as we count on life to be completely rational, there are many paradoxes that we live with all the time. In quantum physics, for example, light behaves as both a particle and a wave. Failure often leads to success. The idea of finding a diamond at your rock bottom is a paradox. The paradox has a spiritual quality since it is not completely rational. To believe in something that does not make total sense takes faith and a certain level of spirituality.

However, Western culture does not place a high value on spirituality. It tends to value thinking, logic, and reason more than faith, intuition, and mystery. The latter are often downplayed, if not ignored and ridiculed. We humans have this ego delusion that we can figure out all of life's problems through logic and reason. Carl Jung was under no such delusion—he believed that we can never solve the major problems of life with our logical, analytical minds because these problems are beyond the limits of human reason. He valued the paradox because it recognizes the limitations of our human knowledge.[3]

People do not value paradoxes because most limit the function of their mind so that it cannot hold two competing opinions. Instead of always thinking either/or, ask yourself if both things can be true at once. You need to expand your mind to be able to hold space for concepts that seemingly contradict. It is only then that you can connect the dots and find patterns that other people overlook. Author F. Scott Fitzgerald, in his book *The Crack-Up*, punctuated the importance of this concept when he said, "The test of a first-rate intellect is the ability to hold two opposing ideas in your head at the same time, and still retain the ability to function."

Your need for certainty is holding you back. You need to let go of certainty to find your diamond. Wrestling with opposing ideas in your mind is where the real growth occurs. It's uncomfortable, but growth is always uncomfortable.

Paradoxes illustrate the limits of human knowledge because they challenge our assumptions about the world and expose the contradictions that come from them. They force us to think deeply and creatively about fundamental concepts such as truth, identity, and the nature of reality, revealing the gaps and inconsistencies in our understanding. Ultimately, paradoxes teach us humility, encouraging us to embrace the complexity and mystery of the world and to be open to new ideas and experiences.

CHAPTER SUMMARY

- Replace limiting beliefs in your subconscious by changing your words and self-talk.
- Use this change to rewrite your narrative and transform your identity.
- Embrace the uncertainty and paradox of not knowing who you are
- View an "identity crisis" as a chance to redefine who you are.
- Commit to becoming your highest self and shaping your unique path.

PART II

Enhanced Spiritual Development

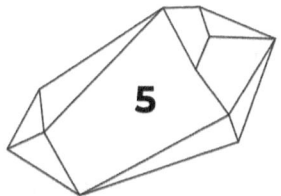

YOU MUST GO INTO THE WILDERNESS

"Everyone thinks of changing the world, but no one thinks of changing himself."

—LEO TOLSTOY

In the past few decades, a new form of psychotherapy has emerged: wilderness therapy. The basic idea is to take teenagers and young adults on a guided journey into the wilderness, where they do not have access to their phones, TV, or electronics and they go through exercises with trained therapists. These programs last anywhere from a few days to several months. One program, Open Sky Wilderness, has listed on their website that the areas of impact of wilderness therapy include the capacity to thrive, overcoming adversity, healthy living, family connection, rite of passage, and the student pathway.[1] Programs like this take participants on a journey of self-discovery, from which they emerge as changed individuals. The idea sounds far-fetched at first, but it fits into a larger pattern that goes back centuries.

For hundreds of years, humans have recognized the transformative power of the wilderness. Many ancient cultures had boys go into the wilderness as a rite of passage into manhood. Even Jesus Christ had to spend forty days in the wilderness and be tempted by the devil before he could begin his ministry. The wilderness, in many narratives and philosophical traditions, represents a place of testing, solitude, and potential growth. However, this concept is not just physical. The physical wilderness is often a path to a psychological wilderness. Whether physical or metaphorical, we must all go through some sort of wilderness journey to be able to reach our true potential.

We all want to fit in with others. We all want other people to like us. It's only natural, because thousands of years ago, other people liking us was the difference between death and survival. Access to food, shelter, resources, and protection from dangerous animals and weather hinged on how well we could get along with the group. This is not quite the case now in the twenty-first century. While it would be nice for everyone to like us, it's no longer the difference between life and death. The problem is that some of us still act like it is. This importance we place on being liked is a manifestation of our innate need for belonging.

True Belonging

We all have the desire to belong to a group. In her book *The Gifts of Imperfection*, Brené Brown defines belonging as wanting to be included in something larger than we are. A major issue occurs, however, because we try to achieve belonging by seeking approval and fitting in, which are not the same as belonging.[2]

> **Because *true belonging* only happens when we present our authentic, imperfect selves to the world, our sense of belonging can never be greater than our level of self-acceptance.**

We all want to be a part of something bigger than ourselves. But at what cost? We are so afraid of people judging us, so deathly afraid of what people think about us, that we hide our true selves and pretend to be someone we're not, just so we can fit in. Belonging is important, but the price is too high if it costs you being your true self. This can hold us back from achieving our true potential. Nobody ever achieved greatness trying to be like everyone else. Conformity means that you're trying to fit in.

But fitting in is not the same as belonging. You can never experience true belonging unless you can be your full, authentic self. And you'll never have the courage to fully be yourself until you accept yourself. But how can you accept yourself if you don't truly know yourself?

Self-Discovery Through the Wilderness

You must go on a journey of self-discovery to find your diamond, and this pathway leads through your personal wilderness. This is where you're spending time alone to figure out who you truly are. This is where you incorporate everything that we have talked about up to this point—embracing post-traumatic growth, letting go of the illusion of failure, accepting reality, and rewriting your personal story—and let it sit in your mind. This is where you're really digging deeper and increasing the pressure to form your diamond.

As a metaphor, the wilderness usually represents an emotional, spiritual, or physical journey, and it's one that requires solitude and vulnerability. You have to find your own way in the wilderness. The wilderness is where you really find out what you're made of. Brené Brown uses this concept in her subsequent book, *Braving the Wilderness,* to update her definition of true belonging:

> Once we belong thoroughly to ourselves and believe thoroughly in ourselves, true belonging is ours. Belonging to ourselves means being called to stand alone—to brave the wilderness of uncertainty, vulnerability, and criticism.[3]

I love this definition because it gives us the other side of belonging, the side that is not focused so much on others but instead on ourselves. Too many of us try to fit in and belong with outside groups when we don't even belong to ourselves. We don't even feel at home with ourselves. But when we do, there's a world of difference. When we have that security within yourself, the game changes.

Being secure within ourselves is critical to growth, but it takes extreme courage to go into the wilderness. Unfortunately, many of us are so insecure that we practically live for other people's approval. By human nature, people are usually only comfortable with the status quo, and going into the wilderness is anything but that. Since we all have the natural impulse to belong to a group, the idea of being alone or separated from the group is scary enough to keep most of us away from the wilderness our entire lives. The good news is that once we gather the initial courage to venture into the wilderness, the journey gets easier; the hardest part is in the beginning.

You have to learn to accept yourself and believe in yourself to go into the wilderness and complete your journey there. In the wilderness, you will experience vulnerability: it's just you and the elements. There's nothing to hide behind. So you need to learn how to trust yourself. You will need to tackle any and all forms of self-doubt, self-hate, and self-sabotage.

Be Comfortable in Your Own Skin

When you journey long enough and you reach the heart of the wilderness, you'll see that there are many people already there. The wilderness is where all the risk-takers, artists, innovators, and free thinkers live—and they are thriving, creating, and building. One thing they all have in common is that they are comfortable in their own skin. They are other people who are on a similar path. You need to use discernment and learn how to trust these kindred spirits as well.

Some people who have not gone through their own wilderness journey may try to save themselves from the hard work of self-examination by dragging you down with them. Practically, this means that in the wilderness, you will experience criticism from other people. People who don't understand your path will always criticize your decisions. People will always try to put *their* limitations onto *your* life. When people think something isn't possible for *them* to do, they will tell you it's impossible for *you*. They don't want to face their own shortcomings. If they acknowledge that you are able to do something great and they are similar to you, they will be forced to admit that they could do it as well. They don't want to face the fact that they could be doing more with their lives, so they criticize you. However, it may come in the form of advice that is supposed to be helpful. You'll only be criticized by people who are doing less than you, not those who are doing more than you.

Finding the Wilderness

What does the wilderness look like? What are some practical examples of the wilderness? Braving the wilderness could look like proposing to your girlfriend at twenty-seven, even when most of your family questions your decision and tells you that you're too young. The wilderness could be starting a business when you already have a successful career and having those closest to you not support your new business. The wilderness could be deciding to focus on reading, learning, and self-development while those closest to you are mainly concerned with partying and being cool. It could be starting a new podcast without having much of an idea of what you're doing and eventually inspiring countless others to do the same. Although these are all examples from my life, any situation in which you have to stand alone with your idea, business, decision, or point of view is the wilderness.

To truly belong to ourselves and our world, we don't need to *change* who we are—we need to *be* who we are. The truth is this:

> **"In order to have what you really want, you must first be who you really are."**
> **—Tim S. Grover**[4]

And Grover would know, since he has trained world-renowned athletes such as Michael Jordan and Kobe Bryant.

Obviously, this is much easier said than done. Our fear of being alone, our fear of being rejected, and our fear of other people not liking us are all holding us back from making this transition. But the path to true fulfillment requires authentic self-discovery.

Here are some ways you can begin your wilderness journey. You don't have to do all of them, but the more you do, the better.

- Completely log off social media for a few months: Instagram, YouTube, X, TikTok, etc.
- Cut out all nonessential social outings: parties, group hangouts, networking events, etc.
- Cut out all TV, movies, and especially the news. It has more of an influence than you realize.
- Start reading personal development books (like this one!). Don't just read them to read, but read to understand them and apply them to your life. I find that reading in the morning works best for me, but everyone is different.
- Journal consistently. Ask yourself those questions you've been avoiding. Evaluate your relationships, your career, your goals, and your priorities. Really spend time with yourself. You'll be surprised what you find. This will help you distinguish between other people's voices and your own inner voice.

Do Your Own Thinking

If you are ever going to create your diamond, at some point, you must stop pretending. There will eventually come a time when you have to choose between self-betrayal and staying true to yourself. On the journey to digging out and shaping your diamond, there will *always* be a decision point. With one choice, there is the well-worn path of people-pleasing: seeking others' approval, constant worry, fear, and anxiety about what other people think. On the path less traveled, however, you have to pave the way yourself. Filled with darkness and uncertainty, there are no guarantees. You don't know what's around the corner. The only guarantee is staying true to yourself. Only one of these paths will lead you to your diamond. Choose wisely.

> **The value of the wilderness is that you shut off all the inputs that influence you, your beliefs, and your decision-making; you are all alone with your own mind.**

This is the only way to figure out who you really are. This will force your mind to do its own thinking. When you don't have any feedback from the outside world on your thoughts and opinions, you can think much more clearly.

Being in the wilderness will help you listen to your inner voice, find wisdom, develop your own philosophy and identity, and grow your intellectual curiosity. How can you listen to your own inner voice when you're constantly listening to the news, politics, and the latest gossip? All of these loud noises will distract you from hearing your quiet inner voice.

When you are able to get quiet and silence all of the chatter of other people's voices, you will suddenly have ideas from your inner voice that bubble up like pockets of air inside water. They are buried so far down in your mind that it takes deep work to find them, and it is only when that air reaches the surface that it enters your conscious mind. Your inner voice comes from your subconscious mind (see Chapter 4), and it will guide you in how to deal with the world. But only if you can get quiet enough to listen to it.

Your inner voice will also guide you toward wisdom. You need to pursue wisdom as if it's gold. Proverbs 16:16 in the Bible says, "How much better to get wisdom than gold, to get insight rather than silver!" Don't be afraid to ask or pray for wisdom. Psychologists have defined wisdom as the ability to accept multiple perspectives, to respond nondefensively when challenged, to express a wide array of emotions in order to derive meaning, to critically evaluate human truths, and to become aware of the uncertain and paradoxical nature of human problems.[5] Wisdom is timeless truth. Knowledge is knowing what to say; wisdom is knowing when to say it.

We need to use this wisdom to develop our own philosophy of life. We need to take the mental models we have formed to interpret life and test them in the real world, by ourselves. Most of the time, we seek too much social reinforcement with our views and beliefs; we're constantly searching for approval instead of thinking for ourselves. As a result, we rarely journey alone long enough to forge an identity based on validation from within ourselves. The best part about the wilderness is that the social validation is absent. Constantly seeking external validation is one of the biggest ways that we undermine ourselves. We shouldn't t seek validation for what we already know is our truth.

One important aspect of the wilderness is we learn to validate ourselves and be comfortable *without* our views being socially reinforced. This will help us find those activities that we are intrinsically motivated to do. This means that we do something for its own sake (intrinsic motivation) and not because we expect any kind of reward or validation from an outside person or group (extrinsic motivation). The major difference between the two approaches is that intrinsic motivation is much more powerful and sustainable than extrinsic motivation. Focusing on intrinsic motivation means that we think for ourselves instead of looking for outside approval.

The wilderness may be the most difficult part of creating and finding the diamond at your rock bottom. But the highest pressure creates the hardest diamonds.

CHAPTER SUMMARY

- Quiet the external noise to focus on your true identity.
- This focus will lead you on the necessary wilderness journey.
- Attain true belonging by embracing your authentic self, both individually and within groups.
- Self-acceptance is crucial for living authentically.
- Enhance self-knowledge to cultivate self-acceptance, which is the key benefit of the wilderness journey.

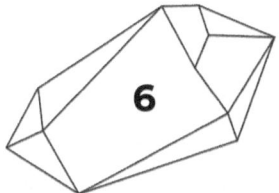

THE ANSWER IS TO QUESTION EVERYTHING

*"The wise man questions himself,
the fool questions others."*

—HENRI ARNOLD

"Have you ever questioned the nature of your reality?" This is the opening line in the TV show *Westworld*, and we would all be wise to ponder the nature of our reality. For those who have never seen the show, it followed the journey of very human-like robots in their journey to achieve consciousness. Each robot was programmed to behave a certain way based on the backstory and narrative that were created for them. They would repeat the same habitual behavior loops and repeat the same patterns, over and over, without questioning. It was extremely appropriate that a robot pondered this question as the first step on their journey to becoming fully conscious and truly alive.

Many of us are just like these robots. We have our backstory. We have our narrative. And we continue to repeat the same patterns of behavior. Never questioning anything, we just run on autopilot. When we are driven by this unconscious behavior, we are no better than robots. **The truth is that we must all question our own reality before we can achieve real consciousness.** Otherwise, we will continue to repeat the same loops and the same patterns, just like robots. Our habits, our current environment, and our internal narrative have too much momentum. Something has to break our pattern. Questions are the answer.

Curiosity is the foundation of the personal growth needed to create your diamond. You have to ask the right questions to start the process of post-traumatic growth after reaching your rock bottom. You have to ask yourself, "How can I make the best of this?" instead of "Why did this happen to me?" You need to replace "Why do I never succeed at anything?" with "What can I learn from this?" Exchange "How can I ever recover from this failure?" with "How can I use this to grow and get better?"

You must be careful of the assumptions that lie underneath the questions you ask yourself. By asking the question in a negative way, you are accepting the premise of the question as true. The fact is that becoming curious and asking the right questions will open your mind up to possibilities you never knew existed.

Questions Create Pressure

You need to assess your current circumstances and determine if they are conducive to creating your diamond. The way to do this is through inquisition. You need to question everything: behaviors, relationships, beliefs, and fears. Why you did certain things. Why you avoided doing certain things. If you say, "That's just how I am," you'll never find your diamond. That phrase is for lazy people who don't want to change and don't want to grow. And that's not you, because you picked up this book. Think about why you are that way. Think about what caused it. Maybe it was something in your childhood. Maybe it was a way to deal with trauma. But if it is not currently the most healthy and productive way for you to live, then you know you must change something. You'll never create enough pressure to turn your coal into a diamond if you never question your habits and environment.

A major area for questions is your relationships. You need to question why you attracted certain people into your life. In romantic relationships, people often have a habit of blaming the other person, especially when things do not work out. Although it may be very convenient and satisfying to say, "He was an asshole" or "She was crazy," how does that help a person grow? Someone who puts all the blame for their previous failed relationships on the other person is *not* someone who takes responsibility for their own faults. It's much easier to point the finger at someone else than to take a look in the mirror and realize you and your decisions have been holding you back this whole time. If most of your previous relationships were toxic, that says something about you. You can't attract people to you unless you are on the same energetic level with them. If you keep attracting toxic people, then there is something toxic about you too. On the other hand, what does it sound like to take responsibility for previous relationships? If you have the courage to say, "I wasn't ready to step up," "I wasn't mature enough," "I'm the one that messed it up," "I ran away because I was scared," or "It's my fault for choosing the wrong person," that is taking responsibility.

Questioning your behaviors and relationships is a great starting place, and they can eventually lead you to question your beliefs. Think about why you accept them as true. You may have simply inherited many of your beliefs from your parents. You may also have many beliefs because it's what your friends or your political party believes. Do you have your personal evidence and experience for these beliefs? Or are you simply taking it on blind faith?

The Importance of Critical Thinking

As you begin to question various aspects of your life, it is crucial to adopt critical thinking as a way of life. Everything you do and participate in needs to be open to questioning and evaluation. You should be very cautious of any group of people you belong to that discourages people from thinking for themselves, whether social or political. It's always better to question things and have it lead to a dead end than to be in a group in which the very idea of criticizing a belief or position is tantamount to heresy. **In a world gone mad, the ability to think for yourself is your most powerful ally.** Don't be trapped by other people's dogma; do your own thinking. Go to the source of the belief system, and don't be afraid to ask questions.

One approach to effective critical thinking is the scientific method. Here's how the scientific method works: You *objectively* test several hypotheses (ideas) before coming to a conclusion, and even then, you are still open to new evidence. This will help you determine the truth. The goal is to minimize the effect of any biases on your thinking so you can come to rational conclusions. Confirmation bias, peer pressure, and preconceived beliefs can all influence your conclusions. The following flowchart illustrates the scientific method.

THE SCIENTIFIC METHOD

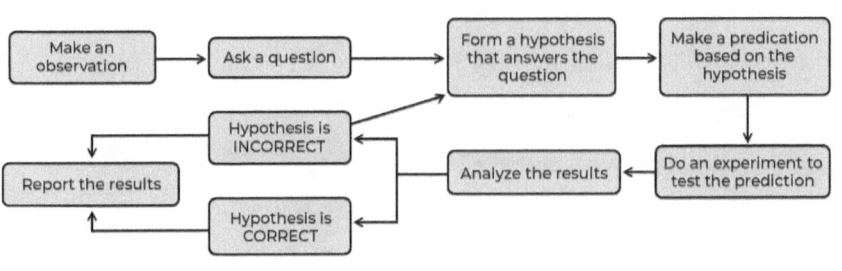

6.1 *The Scientific Method*

Barriers to Critical Thinking

One major factor that stands in the way of critical thinking is a lack of intellectual humility. The researchers who pioneered this term and the framework behind it define intellectual humility as the "nonthreatening awareness of one's intellectual fallibility."[1] In other words, you are aware that you are not always right, and this fact does not threaten you.

Intellectual humility is foundational to critical thinking. The opposite of intellectual humility is intellectual overconfidence, which is exactly what it sounds like. People who think they're never wrong exemplify this. On the other hand, intellectual humility results in the following:

- Respecting other viewpoints
- Not being intellectually overconfident
- Separating your ego from your intellect
- Being willing to revise your important viewpoints

Another factor that limits critical thinking is the social pressure to think like those around you. When groups prioritize reaching a consensus at all costs, this almost always occurs without critical thinking and assessing alternatives. In psychology, this is a phenomenon known as *groupthink*. You can see this in politics quite often these days. The extreme nature of the political landscape and binary thinking enshrined by our two-party system mean that even the slightest questioning of any party position automatically suggests that you must be working for the other side. Clearly, critical thinking is lacking in politics and has been overpowered by blind party loyalty.

The Space Shuttle *Challenger* tragedy in 1986 was another example of groupthink. The shuttle exploded, and everyone aboard died due to mechanical failure, and the worst part is that it could have been avoided. The engineers knew there were mechanical issues, but they wanted to avoid group conflict, so they went ahead with the launch anyway.[2]

Question Your Fears

You need to question your fears. Think about what you are truly afraid of. Think about what is truly the worst thing that could happen. Are your fears based in reality, or is it just an old story you keep telling yourself? Are any of your beliefs limiting you and holding you back? Danger is real, but fear is optional. These are all things to think about.

An old story that encapsulates these ideas tells of an elephant that was being held by a small rope tied to a small stake in the ground (see Figure 6.2). Obviously, this enormous and powerful animal could have broken free at any moment. But it never did. Why was that? The trainer explained that when the elephant was much younger and much smaller, its owners used the same size rope to hold it back, which it did. But as the animal grew bigger, it was still conditioned to believe it could not escape because the rope was holding it back. So it never broke free. This story exemplifies many of us with our fears and limiting beliefs. We can break free at any time, but we are still conditioned to believe that we are held back by these beliefs.

6.2 *Tied Elephant*

Retain Your Childlike Curiosity

Too many of us have an intellectual laziness that inhibits us from asking questions. However, it's not entirely our fault. We are born to be curious by nature, but many of our parents and teachers discouraged us from asking questions in our childhood. Think about all the times we asked one of our parents, "Why?" and they replied with, "Because I said so" or something similar. That is a prime example. We learn very early on not to ask questions, not only by being punished and reprimanded but also based on how we are rewarded. Most of the time, in our school systems, we are rewarded for having the right answers, not having the right questions. To paraphrase an ancient Chinese proverb, **countless people are so afraid of *looking* foolish for a few minutes by asking a question that they risk *being* foolish for the rest of their lives by not asking questions.**

One major problem is that individuals are too concerned with looking cool in front of other people and being like everyone else. The fact is that nobody ever achieved anything great by trying to be like everyone else. Your superpower is that no one else is you. You need to find and embrace what's unique about yourself and use that to create your diamond.

Break Free From the Matrix

In the movie *The Matrix,* the main character is Mr. Anderson, a computer programmer/hacker who also goes by the name Neo. Eventually, he meets Morpheus, who reveals that Neo has been living his life in an artificial simulation and offers to show him the Matrix, which will show him the truth of how the world really is. Neo is presented with a choice, which is not unlike the choice that we are all faced with. The two choices are symbolized by two pills: the red pill and the blue pill. If he chooses the blue pill, Neo will continue the delusion, wake up at home again, return to the simulation, and remember nothing. If he chooses the red pill, his eyes will truly open, and he will see the truth of the world for what it is.

The majority of us are living our lives in the Matrix, and we realize that there is more out there. Yet we choose the blue pill and remain in our comfortable delusion, in an unconscious simulation of the life we could live.

Don't just live your life in the Matrix like everyone else. Take the red pill. See the world for what it is.

Do you just accept things as they are? By questioning authority, traditions, values, cultures, and paradigms, you can break free of the artificial limits that have been placed on you. Don't let your mind limit you. The only limits are the ones that you place on yourself.

An anonymous quote puts it perfectly: **"The mind that perceives the limitation, is [in fact] the limitation."** The only limitations are the ones in your mind. If no limits are allowed, then no limits exist. There are no limits.

CHAPTER SUMMARY

- Starting the journey of post-traumatic growth to find your diamond requires you to cultivate curiosity by asking the right questions.
- Question the nature of your reality to achieve full consciousness.
- Examine your fears, beliefs, relationships, and behaviors.
- Take the red pill to break free from the Matrix that traps many of us.
- Recognize that this is just the beginning of the journey.

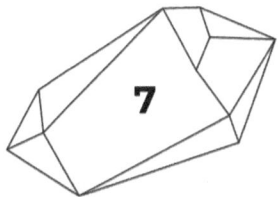

7

DETERMINE YOUR VALUES

*"It's not hard to make decisions when
you know what your values are."*

—ROY DISNEY

In April 2023, Bud Light partnered with transgender influencer Dylan Mulvaney. Mulvaney is a young progressive transgender woman who is known for her advocacy for LGBTQ+ rights. The partnership was controversial because the average Bud Light drinker is a middle-aged conservative cisgender man. This mismatch in values led to a backlash from conservative customers and a significant decline in sales.

Bud Light's decision to partner with Mulvaney was a mistake because the values they were trying to portray with the partnership were different from the values of their average customer. In turn, they failed to anticipate the potential backlash from conservative customers. Bud Light's branding is traditionally associated with masculinity and traditional values. By partnering with Mulvaney, they sent a message that they were no longer a brand for everyone. The backlash against Bud Light's partnership with Mulvaney was swift and severe. Conservative politicians and pundits called for a boycott of the beer, and right-wing media outlets ran negative stories about the company. Bud Light's stock price also took a hit, losing over 10 percent of its value in the days following the controversy. In the end, Bud Light's partnership with Mulvaney was a costly mistake. The company lost sales, alienated its core customer base, and damaged its brand.[1]

Live According to Your Values

This story is a cautionary tale about the importance of knowing and acting on your values. If Bud Light had made a decision based on their brand values, they almost certainly would have made a different decision. Similarly, to discover your diamond, you have to make decisions in line with your values. What kind of person do you want to be? What kind of legacy do you want to leave behind? What do you want people to say about you when you're gone? These are questions that we all need to consider on the search for our diamond. Because the answers to these questions are different for everyone, it's important to take time to think deeply on these matters.

It is paramount to determine your values. Your values are your core principles in life. Once you know your values, you can live a clarified life. Determining your values is critical because it makes every decision in your life a hundred times easier. We will be faced with difficult decisions in our lives. Using your values as a decision-making framework makes things much simpler.

To discover your diamond and live in line with your values, you need to live your life in a way that minimizes regret. One great approach I use to make tough decisions is to think about which choice I will regret more in five or ten years, then make the *opposite* decision. When you decide based on what you value more, ninety-five times out of a hundred, you won't regret it. Regret can be an extremely powerful motivator for our actions if you leverage it correctly by factoring potential future regret into your decisions.

In the context of decision-making, regret often arises when we fail to act in accordance with our values. Regret can also come from not pursuing our dreams and aspirations. By making decisions aligned with our passions and goals, we reduce the likelihood of missed opportunities. **When we make values-based decisions, we won't have regrets in the end, because we will have stayed true to ourselves and who we wanted to be**.

While considering the economic ramifications of a particular course of action is important, too often we fail to think about the intangible consequences of a decision. When we make our decisions, we need to consider not only the immediate cost but also the second- and third-order consequences of that decision. While the cost of something is tangible and/or economic, anticipating the second-order consequences of the decision depends on what we value.

For example, let's say you have a goal to work out four times per week because you value physical fitness. One day, you decide to skip a workout since you had a really long day at work. The cost is that you will miss out on the benefits of working out that specific day. It is more difficult, however, to realize that the second-order consequence is that you are developing the bad habit of skipping the gym, and the third-order consequence is that you are developing the bad habit of breaking commitments to yourself. If you value discipline, consistency, and keeping commitments, then the ultimate cost of skipping a gym day is actually quite high for you, while it may not be a big deal to others. This is because they don't value what you value.

You need to act in accordance with your values to maintain your integrity. You need to lead a life of integrity to create a pure diamond. In the end, you must think, "What do I want to stand for? What kind of values do I want to instill in my (future) kids?" Mahatma Gandhi believed happiness could be achieved when everything you think, say, and do is in harmony, and I would argue that this is also a great definition of integrity. When your actions, thoughts, and words all line up, your life is in alignment. I call this a *congruent life*.

The benefits of a congruent life are immense. Not only are you more at peace and more satisfied, but you also get more joy and more fulfillment out of life. A big source of guilt for many people is not "walking the walk." When what you say and what you do are not in congruence, it can result in *cognitive dissonance*. This is a psychological term that describes the mental discomfort a person feels when they have conflicting attitudes, beliefs, or behaviors. This usually leads to the person changing one of the beliefs, attitudes, or behaviors to reduce this "friction."[2]

How to Determine Your Values

How can you determine your values? One way is to think about the people you admire the most and why you admire them. Chances are, something about the way they live their life aligns with your values. Another way is to think about the times you've felt the most alive and think about those situations. More than likely, something about the circumstances was in line with your values. You can also just think about life lessons that you want to teach your kids, because parents always try to pass their values down to their kids.

It's also a good idea to write your values down. That way, you can save it and refer back to them later, especially as you make important decisions. Regardless of the method, you want to think about what gives your life the most meaning and allows you to give your highest contribution to the world. Those are your values.

When your behavior lines up with your values, you can also maintain your self-respect. When you maintain a fidelity to the vision you have of yourself, you can be proud. Think about if in ten years you will be able to look back on the person you are today and say that you're proud of yourself. If not, then you have an issue with not living according to your values. Regardless of the person you are today, it's never too late to chart a new path.

In five years, you want to be able to look back on yourself and be proud of the actions, behavior, decisions, and habits that you've maintained over the previous five years.

You need to chart a course and create a vision for your life. Maintaining this level of intentionality and consistency in your lifestyle and life design is crucial to discovering your diamond. You need to have your values in mind when you make all of your decisions.

Values-Based Living Is Authentic

So often, we act on impulses and fleeting emotions, without considering the bigger picture of who we want to be and where we want to go. We try to impress others at the cost of betraying ourselves. We overspend our budgets to maintain a false image, at the expense of missing our long-term financial goals. We pretend to be someone we're not in an attempt to gain romantic love, but at the price of losing ourselves. We are so concerned about what other people think that we end up doing things only because we think it's what we should be doing—all while being miserable on the inside.

The truth is that many of us are living inauthentic lives. What is an inauthentic life? As author Eckhart Tolle said, "Living up to an image that you have of yourself or that other people have of you is inauthentic living." When we get so focused on living up to a self-imposed or external image, we miss out on what we truly value and desire. If we're still trying to be someone that we're not, we won't be connected to our true desires. Instead, we need to focus within and listen to our own inner voice, and that will tell us what our values are. Being authentic with ourselves and others will help us find our values.

Framework for Authentic Confidence

Authenticity and vulnerability are required to transform yourself from unrefined coal into a diamond. I have developed a four-step framework that you can use while determining your values. It starts with vulnerability and ends with confidence: Vulnerability leads to authenticity, which will give you courage and then finally confidence. (See Figure 7.1.) This may not make sense on the surface, but allow me to explain. Let's start by defining vulnerability.

AUTHENTIC CONFIDENCE

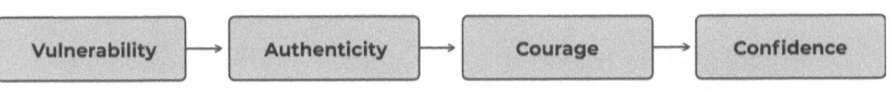

7.1 *Authentic Confidence*

Author Mark Manson defines vulnerability as "consciously choosing to *not* hide your emotions or desires from others."[3] You put yourself out there, no matter the consequences. You just express yourself freely—thoughts, feelings, wants, and opinions, regardless of what other people think. Vulnerability shapes how you relate to strangers, friends, romantic partners, and even family members. Now, obviously you still need to have a filter and use your judgment, but the basic idea is to not hide who you are or how you feel. If you've ever met someone who lives their life completely at ease, completely comfortable in their own skin, not trying to impress anyone, and not trying to maintain some image, then you can be *sure* this person lives their life with a great deal of vulnerability. Although it's much easier said than done, it's the first step to living an authentic life.

Authenticity is the second step. There isn't anyone who has reached the pinnacle of self-development and achieved self-actualization who isn't living an authentic life. Pretending to be someone else and twisting yourself into knots simply takes too much energy, and you need to conserve your energy to pour into your purpose to create your diamond. The truth is that the biggest energy boost is loving and accepting who you are. **The more comfortable you are in your own skin, the less you need to manufacture the world around you for comfort.**

Once you settle into living an authentic life and you're on the path of self-actualization, it will give you courage, which is the third step. It will give you the courage to be who you truly are—courage to take risks and pursue your dreams. This courage will eventually give you confidence once you take enough action—The confidence to be who you truly are with no apologies, and the confidence to be comfortable in your own skin and not need outside approval. So many people want the end result of confidence without going through the steps of vulnerability, authenticity, and courage. But without the preceding steps, it will be a fake, hollow, and brittle confidence.

Author Ryan Holiday has the best definition of confidence I've ever seen: "Confidence is the freedom to set your own standards and unshackle yourself from the need to prove yourself."[4] The imagery in this quote is so powerful because the need to prove yourself is like a set of chains around your neck. It will weigh you down and restrict your movement when you can instead be free of those shackles. True confidence is a form of liberation.

Once you have clarified your values and used vulnerability to lead an authentic life with the courage to be confident, you can make significant progress in the journey of self-actualization. There are many steps required to create the pressure that will take you to the self-actualization that will form your diamond. I have included a helpful graphic from the introduction (see Figure 7.2).

7 STEPS TO SELF-MASTERY

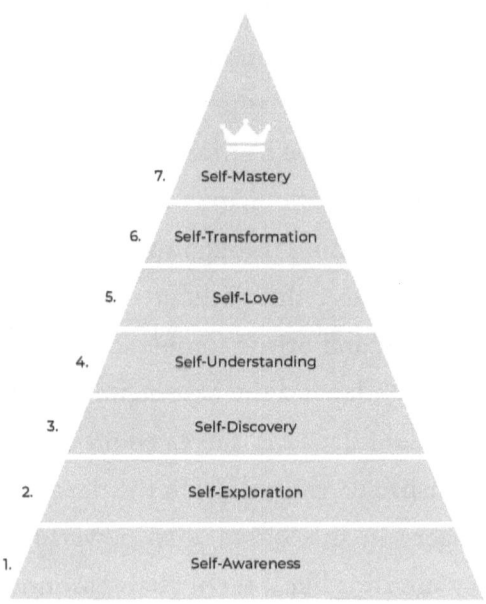

7.2 *7 Steps to Self-Mastery*

Self-actualization requires you to figure out who you are, accept who you are, and transform who you are. You have to love yourself. You have to accept yourself. You have to figure out your values. Psychologist and author Scott Barry Kaufman listed the characteristics of people who achieve self-actualization:

- Truth seeking ("I am always trying to get at the real truth about people and nature.")
- Acceptance ("I accept all of my quirks and desires without shame or apology.")

- Purpose ("I feel a great responsibility and duty to accomplish a particular mission in life.")
- Authenticity ("I can maintain my dignity and integrity even in environments and situations that are undignified.")
- Peak experiences ("I often have experiences in which I feel new horizons and possibilities opening up for myself.")
- Humanitarianism ("I have a genuine desire to help the human race.")
- Equanimity ("I take life's ups and downs with grace and acceptance.")[5]

At the end of the day, you don't need permission to be yourself. Remember that you are the authority on your life. Don't rely on other people, or society, to give you permission to be who you already are. But this does require you to trust yourself. Trusting yourself is much easier when you are on the pathway of self-actualization.

> **You can't trust what you don't know, so if you don't know yourself, you can't trust yourself.**

Just as you wouldn't trust a stranger that you barely know, you won't trust yourself if you are a stranger to your *true* self. On the journey to your diamond, you need to stop second-guessing yourself. Every time you doubt yourself, you are teaching yourself not to trust your own instincts. You will need to tap into your instincts and listen to your inner voice to uncover your diamond.

CHAPTER SUMMARY

- Determining your values is key to finding your diamond at rock bottom.
- Make decisions based on your values to minimize regret and uphold self-respect and integrity.
- Living a vulnerable and authentic life will build courage and confidence.
- The journey of self-actualization can be challenging.
- The next chapter will cover strategies for handling these challenges.

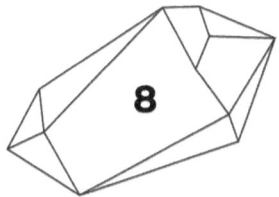

HOW TO STAY RESILIENT ON THE JOURNEY

"The strongest people are the ones who have rebuilt themselves from the ashes of the things that tried to destroy them."

—DANE THOMAS

Meet Dr. David H. Rosmarin. He's an associate professor at Harvard Medical School and the director of the McLean Hospital Spirituality and Mental Health Program. One of his patients a few years ago was a twenty-two-year-old woman who came in with an increase in depression and anxiety. She told him that she was losing hope and didn't think things would ever get better. After some probing by Dr. Rosmarin, she revealed that she believed in God and also thought she had a special purpose on the earth. In just three sessions focusing on these topics, she eventually had increased hope that things could get better, and her depression began to improve.

Similarly, Dr. Rosmarin also saw a Christian man in his mid-sixties who arrived at the hospital with severe depression and marked levels of suicidality. His care team wanted to address his faith but wasn't sure how to do it, so they came to Dr. Rosmarin. The patient revealed that he was in a struggle to pray and think about God in his battle with depression. Dr. Rosmarin then helped him schedule times for prayer and Bible study and urged him to talk to his pastor. After one year, the patient's depression started to improve for the first time in over a year.[1]

If you've hit rock bottom, you may be struggling with your mental health. Anxiety, depression, and even mania are all possible, depending on how you deal with things. Even if you're not at rock bottom, challenges will eventually come. Life always has its ups and downs—you go through a bad breakup, you lose your job, you don't get the job you really want, your business isn't doing well, your kids aren't doing well, or maybe you have health challenges. Regardless of where you are, what is it that will keep you going during the tough times? What is it that will make you never give up, no matter how bleak things seem?

Resilience and Faith

There is a difference between the people who stay stuck at rock bottom and those who rise up and create their diamond. The difference is *resilience*. *Psychology Today* defines resilience as "the psychological quality that allows some people to be knocked down by the adversities of life and come back at least as strong as before."[2]

Post-traumatic growth requires resilience. To create a diamond from your rock bottom, you must be a resilient person. Research has shown that resilience leads to positive outcomes, such as a lower incidence of depression and greater resistance to stress.[3] Dr. Glenn Schiraldi, who is well known for his work on resilience, lists several characteristics of resilient people:

- Sense of autonomy (being self-sufficient)
- Calm under pressure (able to regulate emotions)
- Optimism
- Meaning and purpose (believing your life matters)
- Curiosity
- Social competence (seeking out and committing to relationships)
- Adaptability (being flexible and accepting what can't be controlled)
- *Intrinsic religious faith* [emphasis mine][4]

As you can see, religion is a major factor that increases resilience. In fact, research conducted by Gallup in December 2020 during the height of the global pandemic showed that, at a time when American mental health was arguably at its lowest, the only group to see improvements in their mental health over the previous year were people who attended religious services at least weekly.[5] Research has also demonstrated that belief in God is correlated with improved mental health outcomes in psychiatric patients.[6] Even though we may not currently have this level of mental health challenges, we will all go through various stressful situations. Clearly, religion and spirituality are underrated critical aspects of our mental health.

Since religious belief is associated with increased resilience and resilience has been shown to decrease depressive symptoms, it stands to reason that religious belief can decrease depression. But how would this work? I have created Figure 8.1 to illustrate my framework relating faith, gratitude, and mood.

Faith, Gratitude, and Mood

For those who are not very familiar with graphs of mathematical functions, I will explain. Essentially, the balance between faith and gratitude is what will keep your mood stable. Your faith is the lower bound for your mood—meaning that no matter what, your mood will never go down below a certain point because you always have your faith in God to lean on. Faith essentially means that you believe in something bigger than yourself, and this keeps you from getting too low. Since we will always encounter challenges and we are not infallible, you must trust in something that is infallible. Michael Todd said it best when he stated, "Faith begins where understanding ends."[7] Faith is believing something that doesn't make rational sense. Reason is logical; faith is spiritual.

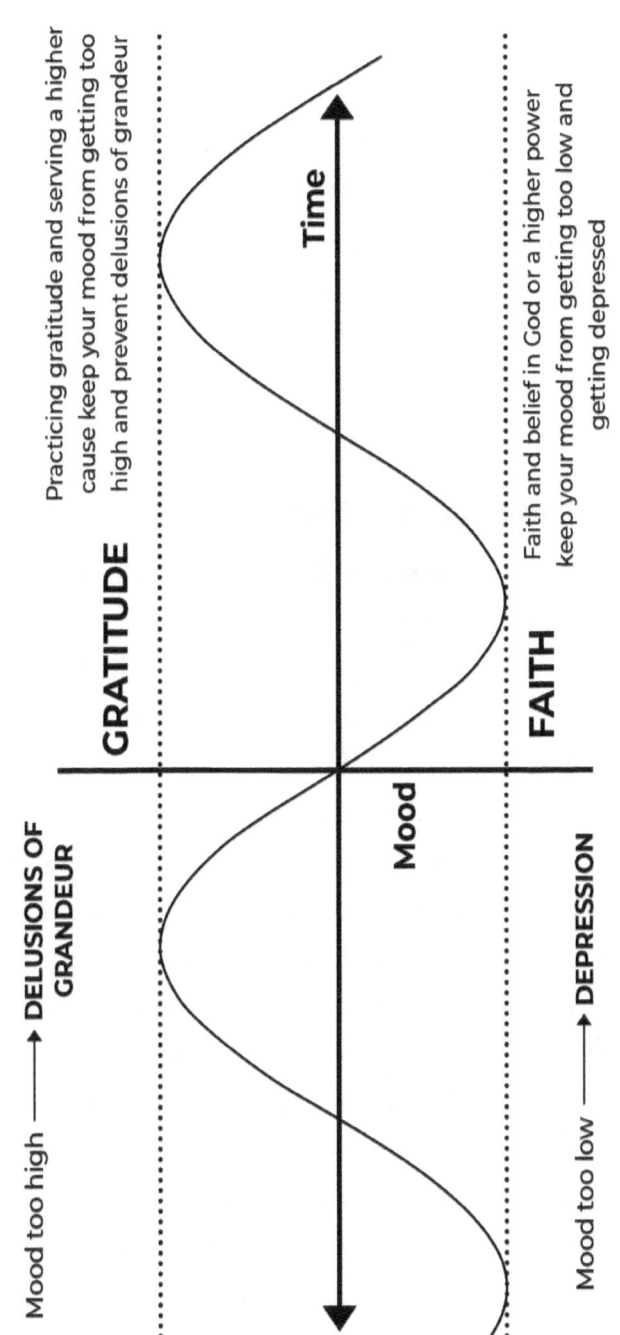

8.1 *Gratitude Scale*

On the flip side, gratitude keeps your mood from getting too high. If you're not grateful for the good things in your life, you'll take them for granted and think that you deserve them. Giving God the praise and the glory for your success creates an upper bound for your mood—you will remain humble, and you won't let success go to your head if you really believe it all comes from God. Gratitude keeps things in perspective.

Religion and Spirituality

However, there's a difference between religion and spirituality. Vine Deloria Jr. made a critical distinction when he said, "Religion is for people who are scared to go to hell; spirituality is for people who have already been there." If you only have religion, it's more than likely because you believe there's a place called hell and you need to be a good person in order to avoid it. However, if you have spirituality, it's most likely because you have been through very challenging circumstances ("hell"). Once you have been through the metaphorical "hell" that is rock bottom, it becomes much easier to have a personal connection to God or the higher power you believe in (spirituality) or to believe in a higher power if you previously did not. As the saying goes, "There are no atheists in foxholes," meaning that everyone believes in God when their life is in danger and they need help. Similarly, if you are at your rock bottom, it's the perfect time to discover or rediscover your belief in God and your spirituality.

Another difference between religion and spirituality is the perspective. Religion is external. Spirituality is internal. Deepak Chopra captured this perfectly when he said, "Religion is belief in someone else's experience. Spirituality is having your own experience."[8] You need to have your own personal encounter with God or the higher power you believe in to be spiritual. Religion is *looking good* on the outside. Spirituality is *being good* on the inside. The two have often been mistaken as being the same, which is why I believe there has been such an effort to distinguish between them.

Religion Versus Spirituality: A False Dichotomy

However, I believe many debates on this topic create a false dichotomy and completely miss the mark. In my perspective, the discussion should not be whether one is more important than the other. Religion *and* spirituality are both necessary pieces of a complete and fulfilling life, and either one is incomplete without the other. Spirituality is extremely individualized, and without religion, it is extremely difficult for it to grow or spread at scale to other people. Without religion, you don't have the external behaviors, structure, or framework to create community and be a vehicle for others to be inspired to have their own personal relationship with God.

But if that's the only thing you have and the spirituality is absent, then there's a problem. If you are one of these people, you have all of the religious external behavior, but in your day-to-day life, you act no differently than anyone else. When nonreligious individuals come close to you, they will see that your religion is hollow and your beliefs actually do not make you a better person on the inside. Consequently, they will become cynical, bitter, and jaded. This is much of the issue with Christianity today.

I would argue that most of the pushback against religion is because most religious people lack spirituality. If religion doesn't actually change people's overall behavior outside of the day they go to worship, then nonreligious people will ask themselves, "What's the point?" If religion actually made people become better human beings all by itself, then people would love religion! However, that's not the case, because you need both spirituality and religion. Spirituality, or having your own relationship with God (or another higher power you believe in), is actually what affects how you live your life and how you treat other people, *not* religion.

> **The truth of the matter is that religion without spirituality most often becomes another high horse that people can sit on and claim moral superiority over others.**

"I'm a vegan, so I'm better than you." "I'm a Democrat/Republican, so I'm better than you." "I do CrossFit, so I'm better than you." "I'm a Christian, so I'm better than you." These are all examples of the same "holier than thou" mindset, which is actually antithetical to the beliefs of most major religions.

Resilience and Your Support System

In addition to religion, another critical factor that can increase resilience is your support system. You need a support system to lean on when things get difficult. Ideally, your support system would be your family, but it can be anyone who wants the best for you, loves you, and is there for you.

Consider the simple act of scheduling weekly coffee meet-ups or setting up routine video calls with friends and family. These regular check-ins create a routine that promotes open communication and trust, making it more natural to seek help during a crisis. They ensure that when you need to lean on someone, the act of reaching out feels authentic, not like a transaction.

CHAPTER SUMMARY

- Just like coal, you must endure significant pressure to transform into a diamond.
- Belief in yourself and a higher purpose is crucial for handling this pressure.
- Faith, a solid support system, and a clear life mission are key to building resilience.

- These factors will empower your transformation.
- The upcoming chapter will discuss how to sharpen your tools to uncover your diamond.

PART III

Creative Growth

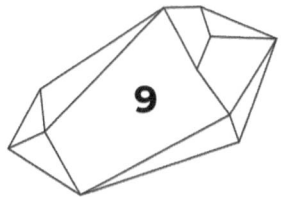

SHARPEN YOUR AXE FOR CUTTING

"If I had eight hours to chop down a tree, I'd spend the first six of them sharpening my axe."

—ABRAHAM LINCOLN

There was once a young woman in New York City named Lily. And Lily loved to cook. She was a dreamer, and she always aspired to be professional chef. However, she often found herself wandering, distracted by the chaos of everyday life, and achieving her dreams felt very far away. She wasn't sure how she could, or even *if* she could, make her dreams into a reality. She realized she needed to practice her culinary skills more, so she decided she would have a series of dinners with her friends where she would invite them to enjoy a meal. She set the menus ahead of time and even let her closest friends make requests for the menu.

For the first menu she decided to prepare a steak stir-fry with rice and an assortment of vegetables. However, when she was preparing the meal, she noticed something odd: The vegetables were very difficult to cut. Also, the steak required quite a bit of force for her to properly chop it, but she wasn't sure why. As she was thinking about this, suddenly, her right hand slipped, and the knife sliced across her left hand. She should have been bleeding. But she didn't even have a cut! Immediately she realized the problem: Her knife was dull!

Fortunately for Lily, she had recently met a famous chef named Chef Marie. And Lily knew that a chef like her would have a great knife sharpener, so she gave her a call and showed up with her dull knife. While Lily was sharpening her knife, she decided to take the opportunity to ask Chef Marie the reason she was so successful. Marie paused for a moment, considering Lily's situation and the best way to impart her wisdom.

"Lily," Chef Marie said, "imagine your skills as the ingredients of a recipe. Your talent, knowledge, and creativity are essential, but to truly shine, you must also sharpen those tools the same way you're sharpening that knife. And the best way to do that is through good habits, discipline, and taking care of your body and mind." A light bulb went off in her head. Lily knew the path to success, and she knew that it would take hard work to get there.

Sharpen Your Saw

Before you start to dig for your diamond, you need to have the proper tools, and they need to be sharp. Stephen Covey popularized the concept of "sharpening the saw," which is essentially taking care of yourself so you can function at your best. While this is important, you need to take it a step further. **To find the diamond at your rock bottom, you need to become the best version of yourself physically, mentally, and emotionally.** This is how you sharpen your axe to uncover your diamond. As Anthony Moore, a blogger on Medium, said, "When you routinely make time to operate at your peak level, your peak level becomes your routine."[1] This could not be more accurate. You need to operate at your peak level or very close to it to discover your diamond. You won't uncover your diamond if you're out of shape, mentally drained, unfocused, and emotionally volatile. You have to work on all of these areas. I will share some key insights that I've learned from my own journey to find my diamond.

One of the first areas to work on is improving your habits. Habits are essentially the brain's way of saving mental energy. Habits are automatic; we do them without thinking. Research has shown that almost half of the behaviors we do every day are based on habit.[2] Therefore, it's vitally important to make sure that your habits are working to your advantage and not to your detriment. Your habits are either your biggest asset or your biggest liability.

> **Either your habits serve you,
> or you serve your habits.**

Take Control of Your Habits

If you are not taking control of your habits, they are taking control of you. You are either building good habits or you are building bad habits—there is no in-between.

When you purposefully cultivate good habits, you can reap the rewards for the rest of your life. It's essentially an investment that will continue to yield dividends into the future. You can think of productive habits as the compound interest that leads to success. F. M. Alexander, an Australian author and actor, stated, "People do not decide their futures; they decide their habits, and their habits decide their futures." If you can automate productive behaviors and basically put them on autopilot, you will be far ahead of everyone else who has not done the same. If you decide to have great habits, you will have a great future. Your habits are what will take you to your destination. Can your current habits carry you to your dreams? If not, you know you need to make changes.

The Mental Benefits of Discipline

The power of having good habits and routines is that it eliminates many of the insignificant decisions that we make on a daily basis. If journaling is one of your habits, you don't have to waste time and energy deciding if you will journal on any given morning. You just wake up and start writing. If you've already committed to a workout schedule, there's no arduous thought process that determines if you will work out on a particular day. You just check your calendar and treat it like a mandatory appointment.

Many people feel like being disciplined and having routines limits you, but in fact, it gives you more freedom. Instead of wasting brain power on small decisions, it allows you to use your limited energy on bigger things. In other words, it frees up your cognitive load. *Cognitive load* refers to the total amount of mental effort being used in the working memory. In practical terms, our brain has a limited capacity to process information and make decisions effectively at any given time. When too many tasks demand our attention simultaneously, or when a single task is overly complex, it strains our cognitive resources, leading to potential errors, increased stress, and decreased efficiency.

For example, consider a professional who starts their day deciding what to wear, which tasks to prioritize at work, whether to go to the gym, and what to eat for lunch, among other decisions. Each choice requires mental energy, cumulatively adding to their cognitive load. By the time they tackle work that requires deep thought or creativity, their cognitive performance might already be compromised. In contrast, establishing routines such as planning meals for the week or deciding work and exercise schedules in advance can significantly reduce cognitive load. This streamlined decision-making process not only conserves mental energy but also enhances focus and productivity on tasks that truly matter.

Automating your habits and routines also takes advantage of a concept called *decision fatigue*. When people have to make a series of choices or decisions over a period of time, the quality of those decisions begins to decline. You can think of your brain as a muscle. Given that every decision you make requires mental energy, it makes sense to conserve that energy for important decisions compared with choices with low stakes. Having habits and routines for everyday decisions makes you more effective. Instead of being focused on the minutiae of everyday life, you can focus on the bigger picture. For example, former President Barack Obama is famous for only wearing a limited number of suits and ties. Steve Jobs was known for wearing his black turtleneck sweaters. In both of these cases, this eliminated the need to decide what to wear every day, so they could conserve mental energy for more important choices.

Another benefit of intentionally developing good habits and routines is that they can give you a sense of continuity and stability when your life changes. The only constant in life is change, so it's always a great feeling to know that your good habits will still remain the same. You can get a new job and move across the country, but you keep the same workout routine. Maybe you get a new girlfriend or boyfriend and you lose a few friends, but you continue to write in your journal almost every day. Over the years and decades of your life, your habits can create an anchor for your life. Without an anchor, when too many things in your life change at once, you can feel like a totally different person. I can only speak for myself, but I know that it was very stressful the few times I felt like everything in my life changed at once. It always felt much more manageable when a few things changed in my life but I was able to maintain my good habits.

Choose Your Pain

Creating good habits is the first step to developing discipline. Usually, "discipline" has a negative connotation. One of the things that stands in the way of developing discipline is the discomfort and pain that comes along with it. **Yes, discipline is uncomfortable and painful, but nothing is worth having in life that's easy and pain free.** Having a healthy marriage is difficult. Building a successful business is difficult. Getting and staying in shape is difficult.

So if we acknowledge that pain and difficulty in life are unavoidable, then the question shifts to what type of pain you prefer. There's the pain of working hard to achieve your goals and reach your potential, or there's the intense agony of missed opportunity and regret that comes from not having discipline. These two types of pain are not the same. Author Jim Rohn agrees and takes it even further a post on X: "We must all suffer from one of two pains: the pain of discipline or the pain of regret. The difference is that discipline weighs ounces, while regret weighs tons."

Mike Tyson is someone who had a lot of discipline, at least when it came to boxing. In an interview on TikTok, he stated, "Discipline is doing what you don't want to do, but doing it like you love it." I love this definition because it captures the fact that you don't always *want* to do what you *need* to do. The fact is that you cannot let how you feel on any particular day sabotage your long-term progress toward your goal. It doesn't matter if you don't feel like putting in the work because you had a bad day. Discipline is about commitment and follow-through. What matters is the commitment you made, and you *must* follow through with it. If you're not committed enough to your goals to put in 120 percent effort, it's fair to question if you really want those goals badly enough in the first place.

Motivation is not enough. Many people have the misperception that if only they were properly motivated, then they would achieve their goals. But the problem is no one is motivated every single day. However, you can be disciplined every single day. Motivation depends on how you feel on a given day. Discipline does not.

> **Motivation is what gets you started, but discipline is what keeps you going.**

Discipline carries you through the days you are not motivated, and those months and years turn into the foundation of your success.

Follow-Through

The most important part of discipline is follow-through. Make decisions ahead of time, and *always* follow through with your decisions. You *cannot* second-guess yourself. Without follow-through, you have no discipline. Without follow-through, you become unreliable, both to yourself and others. People will know that they cannot count on you, and you will know deep down that you cannot count on yourself. Your follow-through must be impeccable. Your mind will try to talk you into procrastination and laziness, but you must win the battle. You must keep the promises you make to yourself so that you know internally and subconsciously that you are a reliable and trustworthy person. This will increase your confidence and self-sufficiency; when you have an idea or a plan, you know on a gut level that you *will* get it done. Period. Conversely, if you have a track record of not keeping the promises you make to yourself, you will already be comfortable with the idea of not executing and giving up because that bad habit has already been formed.

One Path to Discipline: Physical Fitness

How can you develop discipline? One great way is through exercise. I'll give an example from my own life to illustrate. I started lifting weights during my junior year of high school, at sixteen, but I was very inconsistent. Throughout college, I was struggling to adjust and focused on other things, so I only went to the gym whenever I remembered and had free time.

But once I got into pharmacy school and completed my first semester, I decided it was time to get serious. It was about eight years after I started lifting, and I was sick and tired of gaining muscle just to eventually lose it by not being consistent. I realized that I was literally wasting my time in the gym if I wasn't going to be consistent.

So I developed a plan. One of the great parts about being in school full-time is that your days are very regimented, and your classes are on a set schedule. This made it very easy for me to create a set workout schedule and stick to it. I knew what time all my classes, labs, and recitations were, and I put those all on my calendar. I went even further and put my study time in the library on my calendar as well, and my four workout days were appointments on my calendar (and still are to this day!). I had moved closer to campus, so I also factored in the time it would take me to get to and from my apartment. From Monday to Friday, my entire days were scheduled on my calendar.

It may sound unnecessary to some people, but it was highly effective. Not only did I gain twenty pounds of muscle and get into incredible shape, but my grades were also the best they had ever been. I made the dean's list both semesters, which I had not done since high school. This was not a coincidence.

> **When you develop discipline in one area of your life, it naturally carries over to other areas of your life.**

I can confidently say that if you have the discipline to get into shape and stay in shape, you have the discipline to accomplish anything.

Not only is exercise an effective way to build discipline, but it also has countless other benefits that you will need to discover your diamond. It has benefits for your mental health, your physical health, longevity, sleep, and overall quality of life. You feel more confident, and accomplished, you get the boost of endorphins, and it's an amazing stress reliever. In my experience, I've found that most people exercise because they want to look good. There's nothing wrong with this, and it's the same reason that I started. But I've found that the desire to look good is probably not the best long-term motivator for a lot of people. Many times, people will want to look good to show off for a certain occasion (e.g., a wedding or a tropical vacation). But once the occasion comes and goes, their motivation is gone as well.

However, I feel that the mental benefits of exercise are underrated. If you're only exercising for the *physical* benefits, you'll stop once you look like you want to. But if you're exercising for the *mental* benefits, you'll want to feel great all the time. I started working out to *look* good, but I stayed consistent with it to *feel* good.

No discussion of exercise is complete without mentioning nutrition. I won't do a deep dive here, but I'll mention some principles I've noticed that I think can help most people. Nutrition is foundational to good health, and you can't out-exercise a bad diet. The first tip is to avoid processed food as much as possible. A good rule of thumb is that if it didn't exist 150 years ago, you probably shouldn't be eating it much, if at all. The second tip is to increase your fiber to carbohydrate ratio. Fiber slows down the absorption of sugar into the bloodstream so that your insulin does not spike as much, and less of the sugar will be stored as fat in your body.[3] Practically, this means you should significantly increase your fiber intake and cut down your carbs and especially sugars. Some great sources of fiber include avocados, broccoli, kale, and other cruciferous vegetables (i.e., leafy greens). The third tip is that protein is a necessity, especially when you're lifting weights. Protein will help you maintain and increase your muscle mass, and your body has to burn calories to digest it.

The fourth and final tip will be controversial, but I stand by it. Counting calories is not a good use of time. What exactly is a calorie anyway? From physics, a calorie is the amount of heat energy it takes to increase the temperature of one kilogram of water by one degree Celsius. As it relates to food, a calorie is the amount of heat energy released when that food is burned in a vacuum (you can research *bomb calorimetry* for more information on this).[4] A calorie is basically a crude measure of the amount of energy that food contains. The only issue is that the way your body utilizes that energy differs based on your metabolism, your hormones, and the exact macronutrient (i.e., fat, carbohydrate, and protein) makeup of that food.

A concept called *Goodhart's Law* explains the problem with counting calories. Goodhart's Law states, "When a measure becomes a target, it ceases to be a good measure."[5] Calories are simply a measure, but people use them as a target. Once your focus is on calories, you lose sight of macronutrients and other more important factors. Counting calories also makes you more susceptible to thinking you can out-exercise a bad diet.

The Power of Reflection Through Journaling

Once your habits, discipline, and physical health are on the right track, you can focus on your mental and emotional health. One of the most helpful ways to do this is journaling. Journaling is a very powerful tool. Thinking in writing has a magical quality of clarifying your thoughts. In fact, the purpose of journaling is to trap your mind into doing its own thinking. Journaling helps you prioritize, illuminate your thinking, and accomplish your most important tasks instead of urgent busy work. When you journal and reflect on your life, you get to use the benefit of hindsight to assess your previous actions and experiences. By doing this, you can identify patterns in your behavior you may have otherwise never noticed. When you combine action with reflection, you'll take *better* actions over time. It's much easier to turn mistakes into lessons learned when you write about them. In essence, you are having a conversation with your future self when you journal and reflect on it. It's almost like a time capsule on a smaller scale.

Reflection and review help you improve yourself and your habits over the long term because it gives you greater awareness and helps you see ways you can improve. Without reflection, you can make excuses, rationalize things, and lie to yourself. Without reflection, it's almost impossible to determine whether you are doing better or worse compared with before.

One barrier to journaling is that people think they don't need to write things down. Many of us have this ego delusion that our memory is infallible. We don't write things down because, we say, "Oh, I'll remember that." We can't even remember what we had for breakfast three days ago, yet we foolishly think we will remember an idea we had three months later. Some of us have this counterproductive idea that not remembering everything we think of is a weakness, when it's simply the reality of human nature.

> **The fact is that your mind needs to be a generator of high-quality ideas, *not* a storage place.**

You must capture your thoughts before they escape. Ideas are fleeting. Notions are ephemeral. This is why you must journal.

The power of writing in a journal has at least three benefits directly related to personal growth and discipline: (1) It engages you in a regular practice, so you're forming a good habit. (2) It allows you to express yourself and also work on your writing skills, which can manifest itself in future endeavors (such as writing a book!). (3) When you write something in your own words, it has a special power in it: You have to take your own advice. *What kind of idiot wouldn't take their own advice?* All of these factors will help you on your journey to your diamond.

Journaling will help you create your own safe haven inside your mind. You can always go there no matter what happens in your life. This will increase your resilience and help you deal with difficult situations. When you don't have a safe place in your own mind, eventually you will start to run from yourself when things get hard. You won't be able to face the hard facts about your life because you don't have a safe place to process them. If you're not comfortable being by yourself, you will run to other people or other distractions and never truly know yourself. Journaling will help you process low-energy emotions and release them instead of repressing and bottling them up. This requires stillness. Journaling is an important step in being able to regulate your emotions on your own without any external substance.

Another critical tool in the arsenal is therapy. Many of us have unresolved trauma that can only be unpacked by a trained professional, and there's absolutely nothing wrong with this. Unresolved issues from childhood can be a serious hindrance to emotional health and successful relationships. Sometimes we have blind spots that we'll never notice until someone else shines a light on the areas we can't see and examines the patterns in our lives.

Going to therapy is like going to the dentist. Most people can keep their teeth pretty clean by themselves, but at some point, when the plaque and the tartar build up, you won't be able to effectively remove it by yourself. You need the tools and the training of a professional to get those hard-to-reach areas. Nobody really likes to do it, but it's necessary to achieve full health. And of course, after you go to the dentist, you can much more easily maintain the health of your teeth by brushing them and flossing regularly. Similarly, after you've had a significant number of sessions with a therapist, you can much more easily maintain your emotional health by journaling regularly.

CHAPTER SUMMARY

- Establishing good habits and discipline is the foundation for self-transformation.
- Focus on consistent exercise, better nutrition, and regular journaling.
- Incorporate therapy when necessary to aid your progress.
- These practices help you continually sharpen your axe in the pursuit of your diamond.
- Meditation, an important tool in this process, will be explored in the next chapter.

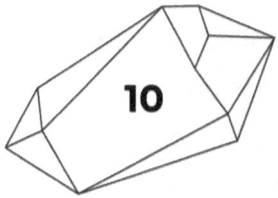

CONTROL YOUR BREATH, CONTROL YOUR LIFE

"Quiet the mind, and the soul will speak."

—MA JAYA SATI BHAGAVATI

In chemistry, there is a concept of the limiting reagent to a chemical reaction. In other words, there is one limiting factor that determines how far the entire reaction will proceed. In the same way, your ego can be the limiting factor determining how far you go in life. Ego, when left unchecked, will ruin you. If you think you're always right, who is going to tell you when you're wrong? There is a certain level of humility and awareness that you will need to uncover your diamond. You will never find your diamond if you are driven by your ego.

There are two things inside of you that you can listen to: either your ego or your inner voice. You can't listen to both simultaneously, because your ego will drown out your inner voice. You have to quiet your mind before your soul can speak. Now, it is true that you need a certain amount of ego to accomplish things. But most people have the volume of their ego up so loud that they can never hear their inner voice. To find your diamond, you must listen to your inner voice; consequently, you must quiet your ego. Scott Barry Kaufman reviewed research on the quiet ego in his book *Transcend*, and the results are very promising. People with a quiet ego have the following:

- **Detached awareness:** With a nondefensive form of attention to the present moment, the individual is aware of the positives and negatives of a situation and attempts to see reality as clearly as possible.
- **Inclusive identity:** With a balanced and more integrative interpretation of the self and others, the person understands other perspectives, allowing them to identify with the experience of others, break down barriers, and come to an understanding of common humanity.
- **Perspective-taking:** By reflecting on other viewpoints, the quiet ego brings attention outside the self, increasing empathy and compassion.
- **Growth mindset:** Quieting one's ego allows for a mindset of personal growth.

When you have a quiet ego, it allows you to consider other people's perspectives, become more aware of the present moment, be more objective, and have a growth mindset. You can observe things from a more neutral perspective and not take everything personally.[1]

If your ego is controlling your behavior, then several things will happen. You will be easily triggered. You will blame other people for your problems. You will be driven by the external validation of what other people think. You will be impatient and always forcing things to work. You will be constantly busy and never at peace.

You need to become aware of your ego and the other parts of your mind, and the best way to do this is to meditate. As Blaise Pascal wrote hundreds of years ago, "All of humanity's problems stem from man's inability to sit quietly in a room alone." This is exactly what you do when you meditate.

Meditation Connects Us to Ourselves

Renowned billionaire investor Ray Dalio attributes much of his financial success to a consistent practice he started long before it became popular: daily meditation. Adopting Transcendental Meditation™ in 1969, six years prior to founding Bridgewater Associates, the world's largest hedge fund, Dalio recognizes meditation as a vital component of his achievements. Dalio's twenty-minute meditation sessions follow a straightforward process. He finds a quiet space, sits comfortably, closes his eyes, and silently repeats a personalized mantra. This rhythmic repetition gradually overtakes other thoughts, leading to a transcendent state in which Dalio describes himself as neither awake nor asleep. Many forms of meditation have the breath as an object of focus rather than a mantra.

Research indicates that meditation can reduce stress, anxiety, and depression, and for Dalio, the benefits extend beyond relaxation. During meditation, he experiences the emergence of innovative ideas, a phenomenon both wonderful and frustrating. Despite the intent to focus on his mantra, creative thoughts arise naturally, akin to the way one gets insights during a soothing shower. Dalio believes this creative surge arises from the subconscious mind, making meditation a conduit for enhancing creativity and gaining clarity for complex decisions.[2]

Now, there is no guarantee that you will become a billionaire by meditating, but meditation is a very powerful practice. What exactly is meditation? Think about how calm and relaxed you feel when you take a deep breath. Now imagine taking many consecutive deep breaths for five, ten, or fifteen minutes every morning before you start your day. In its most basic form, meditation is basically focused deep breathing. Meditation is sometimes perceived to have a religious component, but the majority of the time, people are referring to the physical practice.

I have included instructions on how to meditate here, which are taken from Phil Jackson's *Eleven Rings*:

1. Sit with your back straight and your shoulders relaxed.
2. Bring your awareness to your breath as it moves in and out of your lungs.

3. Allow your thoughts to flow naturally. When a thought appears, acknowledge it, release it, and then refocus on your breath.

4. Rather than attempting to control your mind, let your thoughts ebb and flow naturally. Over time, with consistent practice, these thoughts will drift by like passing clouds, and their influence on your awareness will weaken.[3]

Most forms of meditation instruct you to focus on the breath. What's unique about this is that your breath is your only bodily function that happens autonomously, that you can also control. In other words, breathing naturally happens without you thinking about it (subconsciously), but you can also consciously control your breathing if you decide to. In this way, the breath is the link between what happens consciously and what happens subconsciously.

While your body is engaged in focused deep breathing, your conscious mind has a singular focus: your breath. Your conscious mind is usually active and engaged, so it is typically extremely difficult to access your subconscious. But once your conscious mind is focused on your breath (you can think of it as distracting your conscious mind), you are able to bypass your conscious mind and access your subconscious mind. Other prominent authors and experts also agree.

> **"Meditating is a means for you to move beyond your analytical mind so that you can access your subconscious mind."**[4]
> —Dr. Joe Dispenza

In this way, meditation allows things hidden in your subconscious to come to the surface so that you can become aware of them.

Your hopes, your dreams, your fears, and your hurts all lie in your subconscious mind. Often, certain things that significantly affect a person's come from this part of our mind, and many people go through their whole lives without being aware of them. As Carl Jung stated, "Until you make the unconscious conscious, it will control your life, and you will call it fate." When you consistently meditate, you will be able to make the unconscious conscious so that it does not control your life.

Meditation is a guiding light that pierces through the darkness of our subconscious. It allows us to witness our thoughts and feelings without judgment or attachment. Jung's insight is a wake-up call for all of us to confront our shadows, to illuminate and integrate them into our conscious awareness. This is not easy by any means, but it is a crucial task if we want to control our lives instead of being controlled by fate. In this way, when we control our breath (via meditation), we control our lives. Through consistent meditation, we create a bridge between the conscious and the subconscious minds, enabling us to understand and ultimately transform the patterns that drive our actions.

Furthermore, when you make sure to journal the insights you get from meditation, the power is even greater. In this way, journaling and meditation are synergistic. The act of journaling takes the ethereal thoughts and insights uncovered during meditation and transforms them into concrete revelations. Writing down our experiences and reflections crystallizes their significance.

Meditate for a Better Mind

In order to uncover your diamond, you must become aware of your unconscious mind. **Your highest form will require you to tap into the deepest depths of who you are.** To reach your highest heights, you will first have to become aware of your deepest shadows. Just as an iceberg reveals only a fraction of its mass above the water, our conscious thoughts reveal only a fraction of what lies beneath the surface. Delving into meditation and introspection is like diving beneath the water to explore the vast and intricate structure that influences your life.

Meditation will make your mind work better. It will allow you to perceive your own thoughts, and they will become clearer the longer you stay consistent. Meditation helps you take a step back and look at the big picture, break free from any mental boxes you have created for yourself, and improve your decision-making.

Meditation has numerous proven scientific benefits with regard to positive changes in the brain. It has been shown to enlarge the prefrontal cortex of the brain.[5] This is the area of the brain that is responsible for rational decision-making. Studies have shown that meditation increases gray matter (brain cells) in this region. The great thing about this is that the prefrontal cortex is responsible for self-discipline, willpower, emotions, behavior, judgment, and attention—our overall ability to make choices.

Meditation has also been shown to shrink the amygdala.[6] The amygdala is the part of the brain that is known to be the center for emotions such as fear. Smaller amygdalae, found in people who meditate, have been associated with greater control of emotions. Another positive brain change in meditators is that they have a larger hippocampus.[7] This part of the brain is known to be critical for learning and memory. Research has shown that just a few weeks of meditation increased the size of this brain region.

These findings and other recent research demonstrate that the brain is neuroplastic—meaning the brain can reorder itself by forming new neural connections. This new paradigm of *mental fitness* means that you can train the mind like a muscle by meditating. Just like you can get stronger muscles by going to the gym, you can get a stronger brain by meditating. Meditation, then, is essentially self-directed neuroplasticity—you are using the mind to change the brain.

Researchers have demonstrated that meditation and other breathing exercises (e.g., yoga) promote relaxation by activating the parasympathetic nervous system (PNS) and deactivating the sympathetic nervous system (SNS).[8] The SNS is responsible for the "fight or flight" system in organisms, which raises heart rate, blood pressure, and breathing rate; the PNS acts as an opposite force, promoting the "rest and digest" system, lowering the heart rate, slowing the breathing rate, and increasing digestion. Meditation activates the PNS ("rest and digest") through the vagus nerve (VN). When you breathe slowly and deeply, like during meditation, your diaphragm stimulates your VN. In summary, there is evidence that meditation promotes the relaxation response in the body through stimulation of the vagus nerve.

CHAPTER SUMMARY

- To find your diamond, you must first quiet your ego.
- Meditation is the most effective tool for this purpose.
- It reduces anxiety and stress, enhances clarity, and deepens awareness of your subconscious mind.
- This increased awareness gives you greater control over your life.
- By boosting your "mental fitness" through meditation, you move one step closer to discovering your diamond.

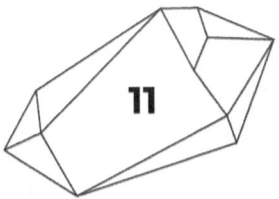

TWO LETTERS THAT WILL CHANGE EVERYTHING

"We all want to say yes, because with yes comes so much opportunity, but with the power of no comes focus and engagement."

—JARED LETO

Meet Marcus. Marcus has always tried to maintain his image as a friendly and caring person, and as a result, he is usually very eager to help others. His colleagues at work and his friends know him as a people pleaser who always says yes to almost every request that comes his way. Marcus is afraid of confrontation and wants to be seen as someone who is always helpful.

One day at work, Marcus's boss asked him to take on a major project. Although he already had a full workload, Marcus couldn't bring himself to say no. He accepted the project, thinking he could manage it alongside his existing responsibilities. Around the same time, his friends asked him to help plan a huge surprise birthday party for another friend, and Marcus was the first one to sign up. Weeks turned into months, and Marcus was juggling work, event planning, and numerous other requests from friends and family. He was constantly stressed and exhausted, but he didn't want to disappoint anyone. Sleepless nights became the norm as his health started deteriorating, and he began to have debilitating anxiety.

As time went on, Marcus began to notice that the quality of both his work and his commitment to the birthday planning were suffering. His girlfriend also noticed that he no longer was able to prioritize spending quality time with her. He was spread too thin, and he felt like he was failing in all areas of his life. Burnout was setting in, and he realized that his inability to say no had led him to this breaking point.

One day, Marcus had a heart-to-heart conversation with his best friend, Steven, who saw the toll his people-pleasing habits were taking on him. His friend reminded him of something Jared Leto said in an interview with *Fast Company*: "With the power of no comes focus and engagement." Marcus realized that by saying yes to everyone, he had lost focus on his own well-being and true priorities.

With newfound courage, Marcus started to say no to additional requests that were beyond his capacity. He informed his boss about his workload and negotiated a more manageable project timeline. He also communicated his need to step back from the event planning committee. Over time, Marcus experienced a positive transformation. He regained his energy and enthusiasm for his work. He nurtured deeper relationships with his girlfriend and the rest of his family by being more present and engaged when he spent time with them. Saying no allowed him to say yes to what truly mattered, and he learned that setting boundaries was not a sign of weakness but a path to a healthier and more balanced life.

The Power of No

You need focus and engagement to uncover the diamond from your rock bottom. Saying yes too easily and too often leads to being overcommitted, shortchanging your relationships, and being unable to reach your full potential.

As Warren Buffet stated so powerfully,

> **"The difference between successful people and really successful people is that really successful people say no to almost everything."**[1]

When you are on the path to uncovering your diamond, you must be so focused on your goals that no becomes your default answer. Every time you say yes to something that's someone else's priority, it takes you away from your priorities. You need to carefully evaluate every request and only say yes when there is a compelling reason. If you are not good at saying no, other peoples' priorities will run your life, and you will not have the time you need for rest and recovery. You will be stressed and burned out, and you won't be able to say yes to the really important things if yes is your default answer. A good no creates room for a better yes.

Think of the power of saying no as a compass that helps you navigate the enormous ocean of requests and opportunities in your life. When you constantly say yes to everything that comes your way, you are aimlessly drifting without direction, and you lose sight of your true goals and values. But when you leverage the power of saying no, you have a dependable compass to keep you on track. Like a sailor using a compass to stay on track with their destination, saying no allows you to stay true to your priorities and values, ultimately keeping you on the path to achieve your dreams and discover your diamond. No prevents you from getting shipwrecked on the shores of overcommitment and burnout. The power of no steers you away from troubled waters and toward the opportunities that truly align with your purpose and vision.

What are some of the reasons that you might yes too easily? Feeling guilty or being afraid of conflict or confrontation is one reason. It could be that deep down, there is a fear that if you say no to someone, you could lose the relationship. This is only ever true in the case of a one-sided relationship, where the other person is using you, and only cares about what you can do for them. That is *not* a relationship worth keeping. Another reason is that you don't want to be rude. There are ways you can firmly but respectfully say no, which I will discuss shortly. Or perhaps you just think that it's easier to go along just to get along, and maybe you can back out of the request later. But this is just kicking the proverbial can down the road, and it looks much worse to back out of what you already agreed to, compared with just saying no in the first place.

However, often the biggest motive for saying yes too often is being a people pleaser. It is natural to want people to like you, but no one can ever make everyone happy all the time. It's a recipe for failure. Either you can constantly say yes in an effort to make everyone else happy and make yourself miserable in the process, or you can get comfortable with saying no and accept the fact that sometimes people will not be happy with you while maintaining your self-respect, values, and priorities.

Here are some practical tips to effectively yet respectfully say no. The first thing is to make sure you are firm in your no. If it's truly 100 percent no, *do not* say, "probably not," "I'm not sure," or "I don't know." Also, try to avoid overexplaining yourself, as this can make you sound hesitant and lead to people trying to push you further to see if you will change your mind. Here are some phrases you can try:

- "I don't have the capacity for that."
- "I don't have time for that, unfortunately."
- "I'm afraid that's not going to fit in my schedule."
- "My plate is already full, so you're going to have to find someone else to help with that. I might suggest _____."

In a work setting, you can try the following:

- "This falls outside of my responsibilities, but I would be happy to connect you with someone who can help."
- "As my workload is quite heavy, can you help me understand what I should reprioritize to accommodate this new task?"

Ruthlessly Prioritize

Along with being able to comfortably say no, you need to be able to effectively prioritize what you have said yes to. To find your diamond, you must be able to ruthlessly prioritize—this means you set your priorities and stick to them no matter what. *Ruthless prioritization* is a concept that emphasizes the importance of making tough choices about where to focus your time, energy, and resources. It involves setting clear priorities and mercilessly sticking to them, even if it means saying no to other opportunities, tasks, or distractions.

Ruthless prioritization starts with having a crystal-clear understanding of your goals, objectives, and what truly matters to you so that you can put those goals first. It's about identifying the few critical tasks or projects that will have the most significant impact. It involves the willingness to say no to activities, commitments, or projects that don't align with your top priorities. It requires the ability to decline opportunities that may be appealing but could divert energy from your primary focus. Businessman and author Robert McKain believed that not prioritizing effectively is the main reason that people don't achieve their goals. Ruthless prioritization means always doing first things first.

Ruthless prioritization often involves identifying and eliminating low-value tasks or activities that don't contribute significantly to your goals. This can free up time and resources for more important endeavors. It also involves establishing deadlines and time limits for tasks and projects, which can help ensure that you stay on track. When done correctly, it prevents procrastination and forces you to focus on what matters most. Priorities can change over time, so it's essential to regularly review and adjust them as circumstances evolve. What was once a top priority may no longer be as crucial, and new priorities may emerge. Journaling is crucial here.

In some cases, ruthless prioritization involves delegating tasks or responsibilities to others who are better equipped to handle them. Delegating frees up your time to concentrate on high-impact activities. Recognizing that prioritization often involves trade-offs is a fundamental aspect of this concept. Life always involves trade-offs. You can do anything, but you can't do everything. You may need to make sacrifices or give up certain things to pursue your top priorities effectively. Ruthless prioritization also emphasizes quality over quantity. By clarifying your priorities and eliminating nonessential tasks or commitments, ruthless prioritization can reduce the stresses that can otherwise overwhelm you. It allows you to concentrate your efforts where they matter most, leading to a more productive, streamlined, and fulfilling life.

Overall, ruthless prioritization is about making tough decisions to allocate your time and energy efficiently and effectively. It's a strategy for achieving your most important goals by eliminating distractions and nonessential activities.

Avoid the Sunk Cost Fallacy

What stands in the way of effective prioritization? Many times, we can't prioritize well because of certain biases we have. The *sunk cost fallacy* is one of those biases. In essence, a sunk cost is an expense that is already gone. We have already paid for it with our money, time, energy, or other resources, and we can't get it back. Oftentimes, the more money or time we have invested into a person, product, idea, or plan, the harder it is to move on.

The sunk cost fallacy is a cognitive bias when a person continues to invest time, money, or resources into a decision or project only because they have already invested a significant amount, even when it no longer makes sense to do so. For example, if you have been in a dead-end relationship for four years but you refuse to leave because that would mean that you "wasted" four years of your life, that is an example of sunk cost fallacy. **The fact that you've already wasted time or money on something is no reason to continue to do so.**

Many people focus too much on sunk cost and not enough on opportunity cost. Opportunity cost is the cost of what you're missing out on by taking your current course of action. With the dead-end relationship example, the opportunity cost is the much better and much healthier relationship you could have with someone else. When making decisions, the future should always take priority over the past. Although you can learn from the past, it's already gone, and it can't come back. Don't forfeit future benefits to justify a past decision. Use your energy for future opportunity rather than obsessing over the past. You can't be afraid to cut your losses. It's okay to admit that you were wrong or you made a mistake.

Important Versus Urgent

A great tool to use for prioritization is called the *Important versus Urgent Matrix*. Originally popularized by Dwight Eisenhower, this important framework captures the truth that what is important is not always urgent, and what is urgent is not always important. I have included Figure 11.1, inspired by Todoist, to indicate what I mean.

	Urgent	Not Urgent
Important	**✓ DO IT** Things with clear deadlines and consequences for not taking immediate action. **Examples** · Finishing a client project · Submitting a draft article · Responding to some emails · Picking up your sick kid from school	**⊙ SCHEDULE IT** Activities without a set deadline that bring you coloser to your goals. Easy to procrastinate on. **Examples** · Strategic planning · Professional development · Networking · Exercise
Not Important	**⊕ DELEGATE IT** Things that need to be done but don't require your specific skills. Busy work. **Examples** · Uploading blog posts · Scheduling · Reponding to some emails · Meal prep · Consider hiring someone or using technology	**🗑 MINIMIZE OR DELETE** Distractions that make you feel worse afterward. Can be okay, but only in moderation. **Examples** · Social media · Watching TV · Video games · Eating junk food

11.1 *Urgency Matrix*

The important thing is not to prioritize your schedule but to schedule your priorities. As an overview, Quadrant I (upper left) tasks are both urgent and important. You want to do these right away. Quadrant II (upper right) tasks are not urgent, but they *are* important. These need to be scheduled and prioritized.

Quadrant III (lower left) tasks are urgent but *not* important. Usually, you will want to minimize your time here and automate, delegate, or batch these tasks. Technology can be useful here for automating, or you can delegate and leverage someone else's strengths, such as those of a friend or significant other.

Batching is another useful tactic. Think about doing laundry. You don't run the washer just for one dirty sock or one gym outfit. You wait until there's enough dirty clothes for a full load, and then you run the machine. Similarly, if you batch your emails, for example, you check your email at preset times and respond to everything rather than replying to every message as it comes in.

Quadrant IV (lower right) tasks are basically time wasters, so consider getting rid of these as much as you can. Doing these activities in moderation, choosing the ones that give you the most joy, and putting strict limits on them tend to be the most effective in my experience. Overall, when any task comes your way, make sure to do it, defer it, delegate it, or delete it. It is also crucial to make sure that your calendar matches your priorities. Furthermore, you want to have a system by which you immediately take one of these actions on anything that comes your way. When you don't have to touch your tasks twice, you can prioritize much more effectively.

CHAPTER SUMMARY

- Learning to say no effectively allows you to focus on what brings the most value to your life.
- Achieve this by ruthlessly prioritizing, avoiding the sunk cost fallacy, and distinguishing between important and urgent tasks.

- These strategies will help you gain better control over your actions and guide you toward discovering your diamond.
- The next chapter will explore how others influence your journey.

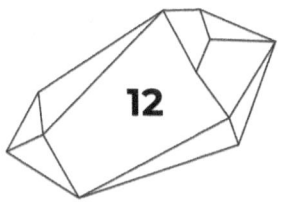

BUILDING BRIDGES GETS YOU FURTHER

"Model someone who has already achieved the results that you want, someone who is consistently successful, because it means they have a strategy. Figure out how they do it. Success leaves clues. If someone is effective not once, not twice, but consistently in anything, they're not lucky; they have a strategy. Study it and figure out what it is."

—TONY ROBBINS

Kobe Bryant was one of the greatest basketball players of all time. Early in his career, he recognized the importance of mentorship and leveraged it as a powerful tool for his personal and professional development. He had a long list of mentors, both on and off the basketball court, who helped him. Jackie MacMullan, in an article for ESPN, wrote about Kobe's mentors extensively during the year that Bryant retired from the NBA.

Although typically most of us will have to seek our mentors, Kobe's biggest mentor actually reached out to him first. Michael Jackson cold-called Kobe in 1997. Apparently, he had been studying Bryant from a distance and noticed they had some similarities. Jackson encouraged Bryant to embrace what made him different and remain obsessed with his craft. Critically, Michael told Kobe that he was mesmerized by the success of the Beatles, and he sought out friendships with Paul McCartney and Yoko Ono to learn more. MacMullan shared a particularly poignant quote that Michael Jackson imparted to the eighteen-year-old Kobe Bryant: "Your curiosity is your greatest gift. Use it to expand your scope. Other people won't understand your insatiable thirst for excellence. They won't bother to keep striving because it's too onerous, too difficult."[1]

Imagine hearing those words from the King of Pop at a young age. Seeing the example that Michael Jackson had studied one of most successful rock bands of all time would be an incredible revelation for someone who is also trying to pursue greatness. At the end of the day, greatness in any field always has common threads. Jackson explained further to Kobe:

> **"You've got to study all the greats. You've got to learn what made them successful and what made them unsuccessful."**

And with this, Kobe had the blueprint to NBA greatness. He combined his unparalleled drive, determination, work ethic, and curiosity with an intentional strategy of seeking out and learning from the legends who came before him.

Later that year, in 1997, he decided to learn from another M. J.: Michael Jordan. Jordan gave Bryant advice on everything from his fadeaway jumper to how to defend bigger players in the post. According to Kobe, "Speaking to M. J. was like getting my own college education at the highest level." This relationship continued over the years, and Kobe began to seek out advice from more of the all-time NBA greats: Bill Russell gave him tips on defense, Magic Johnson taught him leadership lessons, Hakeem Olajuwon taught him post moves, and Larry Bird shared his secrets on preparation and conditioning. Eventually, in his later years, Kobe would go on to mentor another generation of NBA stars: Lebron James, Anthony Davis, Russell Westbrook, Kevin Durant, and Kyrie Irving, among others.

Kobe Bryant's approach perfectly captured the essence of Tony Robbins's statement to "model someone who has already achieved the results that you want." Like Tony says, success always leaves clues. The most efficient path to success involves finding mentors or role models who have achieved what you would like to do. This is exactly what Kobe did. Consistency is a prerequisite for success; therefore, someone who is consistently successful is doing at least a few things right that you can learn from. There is a pattern somewhere, and it's not just luck. If you can put your ego aside (see Chapter 10), you can really achieve exponential growth by actively seeking and learning from individuals who have succeeded in each area you want to improve in. Don't just learn from these individuals either; you must put into action what you learn.

> **Your desire to learn must only be exceeded by your desire to act.**

Networking for Growth

Seeking out mentors and finding valuable relationships are not only beneficial in sports. Meeting the right people and creating the right relationships are crucial parts of discovering and uncovering your diamond. When you are pursuing your purpose, the people you meet along the way can create synchronicity and synergy and expose you to ideas and opportunities you could never have imagined. The fact is you don't know what you don't know. The more you talk to people who are on the path to your purpose, the more your path will be illuminated. Your greatest achievements will usually involve other people, so intentionally networking and building relationships are necessary parts of your diamond journey.

You need to have people around you who you can look to for advice. But it can't just be anyone. The problem with advice is that everyone has an opinion, but few have the qualifications to actually give advice in any given area. It's best to find someone who has the results that you're looking for if you're looking for someone to get advice from. Always pay more attention to people's actions and their results in life as opposed to what they say.

You need to be selective about the people you take advice from. A personal rule of thumb that I live by is this:

> **Do not take someone's advice if you wouldn't trade places with them.**

Since their thinking got them to where they are in their life, if you wouldn't want to be in their situation, it's best not to take that person's advice. If your cousin is giving you financial advice, but you wouldn't trade your financial situation for theirs, it's probably best to (lovingly) ignore his or her advice. As the thirteenth-century poet Rumi said, "When setting out on a journey, do not seek advice from those who have never left home." While, yes, it's *possible* that someone could give you good advice without having the results to back it up in their life, it's not *probable*. Besides, would you really want to risk following bad advice just because there's a *chance* it could be good? It's much better not to risk it.

People naturally want to take the advice of their loved ones, but this can be tricky. Just because someone loves you does not mean they are qualified to give you advice in a certain area. Would someone be qualified to coach football simply because they love football? Of course not, they need experience. However, if you find someone who has a life that you would want, then by all means, take their advice.

Positive Peer Pressure

Don't be a lone wolf. When you intentionally choose to be around people who can help you get to your destination, you will get there quicker. We are all influenced by other people; it's a part of our nature. For example, our brain has mirror neurons that fire to mimic the emotions and actions of people around us. You are the sum of the people you spend the most time with, so select your friends and associates carefully.

I have found that the most successful people leverage the power of positive peer pressure. When you are around other people who force you to level up, you have no choice. When you are around other people who you can both learn from and grow with, it creates a rising tide that lifts all boats. Intentional relationship building will not only increase your odds of success, but you will also enjoy the journey much more. Positive relationships make life richer and more meaningful. Your most meaningful accomplishments will involve other people.

At the end of the day, people are what matter the most. Life is about relationships. Life is about networking. Life is about people. Leadership consultant Margaret J. Wheatley echoes this sentiment when she says,

> **"Relationships are all there is. Everything in the universe only exists because it is in relationship to everything else. Nothing exists in isolation. We have to stop pretending we are individuals that can go it alone."**

This highlights the interconnected nature of existence and emphasizes the fundamental importance of relationships in our lives and in the universe as a whole. We need to acknowledge and value the connections we have with the people and the world around us. The idea of complete independence is an illusion. We cannot exist totally independent of our environment and our interactions with other people. On a physical level, everything in the universe is part of a web of relationships.

These ideas are at the center of Keith Ferrazzi's *Never Eat Alone*. In it, he lays out his philosophy for networking and relationship building, which has been quite successful for him. He debunks the idea of networking as a series of transactional exchanges where people simply hand out business cards. He astutely notes that the best connections aren't the ones where we keep score, but the genuine relationships where each person actually cares about the other person.[2] When you build your network proactively and try to add value to everyone you connect with, the natural consequence is that people in your network will want to help you when you need it.

It's best to think of relationships as long-term investments instead of short-term transactions. Authentic and valuable relationships often take time to develop and maintain. They aren't built overnight. Too often, we have so much of a short-term focus that we don't have the right perspective for lasting relationship success. If you build your network consistently and regularly reach out to people, it won't be that you're only reaching out because you need something.

Overall, it's important to be selective about the people you allow to be in your circle. You want to make sure that you have shared values and a similar purpose. It's only when you want similar things out of life that you can add the most value to each other's lives. It's important to invest in long-term, genuine relationships on the path to discovering your diamond. However, one commonly overlooked feature of good mentoring and networking relationships is to make sure you have the same mindset regarding success.

Abundance Versus Scarcity

There are two types of mindsets when it comes to success: an abundance mindset or a scarcity mindset. As an example, let's say Mary has an abundance mindset. She believes that there are more than enough resources to go around (i.e., abundance). Instead of believing that there are only limited pieces of the proverbial pie, Mary believes that the pie grows and gets bigger all the time. So for this individual with an abundance mindset, another person's success does not equal his or her failure. It only motivates Mary to grow more, work harder, and achieve her own version of success.

An *abundance mindset* is characterized by a focus on possibilities, opportunities, and the belief that there is enough for everyone. It is similar to the growth mindset in that they are both characterized by keeping a positive, open mind. Someone with an abundance mindset approaches friendships and relationships with an open and generous attitude. They are more likely to share knowledge, connections, and opportunities with others because they believe that doing so creates a positive cycle of mutual benefit. This mindset can foster trust, collaboration, and a sense of community. It encourages people to seek win–win outcomes and build supportive, long-lasting relationships.

On the other hand, a person with a scarcity mindset believes the exact opposite. To illustrate this point, let's say Kelly has a scarcity mindset. Kelly believes there are only limited resources to go around (i.e., scarcity). She believes that there are only so many pieces of the pie, so another person's success automatically equals her failure. Naturally, this causes jealousy, insecurity, and many other negative feelings when seeing other people succeed. In my experience, people with a scarcity mindset are the ones who will try to pull you down as you are climbing the ladder of success. As you are on your diamond journey, these people may envy you. They may want you to do well, but *not* better than them. To combat this, make sure you have a strong filter and you are not afraid to cut out negative people from your life.

The *scarcity mindset* is characterized by a focus on limitations, lack, and the fear of not having enough. Similar to the fixed mindset, it has risk aversion, fear of failure, and a resistance to change. As a result, someone with a scarcity mindset may approach friendships and relationships with a sense of competition and the belief that there's not enough to go around. They may be hesitant to share resources, connections, or opportunities with others out of fear of losing what they have. This mindset can lead to mistrust, hoarding of resources, and a reluctance to collaborate. It can strain relationships as people may view others as potential threats to their limited pool of resources.

Evaluate Your Friendships

The varied perspectives that come with an abundance mindset versus a scarcity mindset influence the way a potential friend will act toward you. Therefore, it is best to utilize this information to choose friendships that will become mutually beneficial relationships. When using the abundance versus scarcity mindset as a filter for relationships, there are several factors to consider.

To begin with, assess whether the person shows signs of a scarcity or abundance mindset. Trust is essential in any relationship, and knowing someone's mindset can help you gauge their willingness to collaborate and share resources. Next, you want to evaluate if they operate with mutual benefit in mind. An abundance mindset usually leads to more fruitful and synergistic partnerships. Another important factor to assess is whether there is reciprocity. There needs to be a willingness to give and receive within the friendship, which is more likely with the abundance mindset. You should also consider whether the relationship is geared toward short-term gains or long-term growth. Abundance-minded individuals tend to invest in long-term, sustainable relationships while scarcity-minded individuals may focus on immediate gains. Finally, consider the emotions you experience when you interact with this person. Scarcity-minded relationships may be marked by competition, jealousy, and a lack of trust, while abundance-minded relationships are often characterized by support, encouragement, and mutual growth.

CHAPTER SUMMARY

- Combining insatiable curiosity and a drive for excellence with a strategy of learning from successful mentors will propel you far ahead.
- Success leaves clues, and there is always something to learn from those who are consistently successful.
- Adopting this mindset, while leveraging positive peer pressure and building valuable relationships, puts you on the path to uncovering your diamond.

PART IV

The Identification of New Possibilities and a Purpose in Life

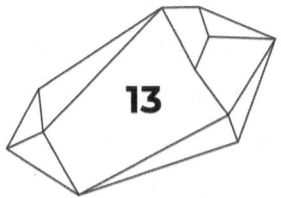

THE POWER IN LETTING GO OF FEAR

"Fear is a reaction. Courage is a decision."

—WINSTON S. CHURCHILL

There is a heavy rope that many of us are holding onto very tightly. That rope is called fear. Fear leads to anxieties, worries, and insecurities that we often carry with us throughout our lives. Many of us believe that holding onto these fears will keep us safe, just like grabbing on tightly to a rope might keep you from falling. However, this is counterproductive, because in the end, you are only hurting yourself.

The more tightly you cling to your fears, the more limited and constricted your life becomes. Holding tightly onto fear will hurt you the same way that holding a rope tightly for too long will damage your hands. The psychological and emotional toll of fear can manifest in various ways, from stress-related health issues to strained relationships. Sometimes, what you fear the most can actually come true *because* you're focusing on it so much. When you fixate on your fears, you give them power. By intensely focusing on what you fear, you can actually attract that very outcome.

The truth is that you get what you focus on, so you should focus on what you want. To find the diamond at your rock bottom, you need to shift your focus from your fears to your desires and goals. The first step in this process is letting go of fear. However, many of us are afraid of falling. But when you let go of the rope of fear, you become free. As you release your grip on fear, you are free to fall into love. Trade your fear for love. Let go of the rope. Release the fear, and fall into love. Once you let go of fear, fear no longer has a grip on you either.

Everyone feels fear, but to reach your true potential, you must make a permanent decision not to act based on fear. You have to "do it afraid" and do that consistently. This transformative commitment means that you intentionally choose to prioritize your growth and development and not let fear stop you.

> **Courage isn't the absence of fear, but the willingness to take action despite fear.**

Fear is the weakest emotion and the lowest energy level you can operate from. But how do you let go and move beyond fear to prevent it from running your life? You have to focus on the opposite of fear, which is love. Elisabeth Kubler-Ross, pioneer psychologist of near-death studies, poignantly describes this dichotomy: "To transcend fear though, we must move somewhere else emotionally; we must move into love."

Kubler-Ross points out the overwhelming benefits of embracing love as a way to rise above the influence of fear. Fear and love are naturally antagonistic to one another, so if you're living in fear, you're not living in love. While you cannot completely remove fear from your life, you *can* make it so that fear is completely powerless to stop you. You have to operate out of love instead of fear: love for yourself, love for others, love of learning, love of exploration, and love of doing what's right.

Emotional Motivation: A Hierarchy

The framework depicted in the following diagram I have created (see Figure 13.1) shows the primary emotional motivators for humans, depicted in hierarchical order on the spectrum of love versus fear. Everyone has a primary emotional motivator, and determining what yours is can help you grow and advance to a higher level. In the diagram, the first thing to note is that the top half of the emotional states is on the side of love whereas the bottom half is on the side of fear. Essentially, the spectrum depicts the positive emotions versus the negative emotions—what you want versus what you don't want. Think about which one you want to focus on. Do you focus on what could go wrong? Focusing on the negative will not prevent it from happening.

LOVE VS FEAR SPECTRUM

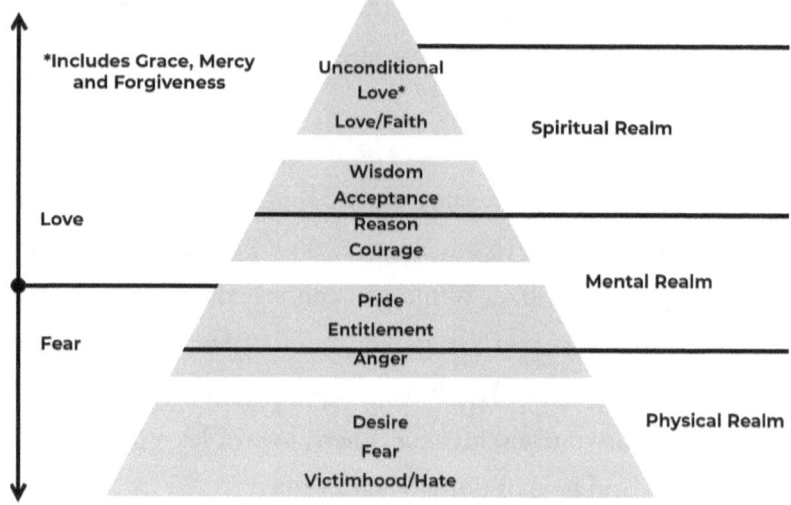

13.1 *Love Versus Fear Spectrum*

Reviewing the spectrum from the bottom in ascending order, we find victimhood and hate at the bottom. In truth, victimhood and hate are two sides of the same coin. On one hand, you have pure, unadulterated hate, which everyone is familiar with. On the other hand is victimhood, which has been falsely elevated as a noble virtue by progressives. Perhaps you may be asking, "What's the connection to hate? I don't get it; it doesn't make sense." The connection is this: If there's a victim, then there's an oppressor. You can't be a victim without an oppressor. To an extent, certain groups (I happen to be one of them) have been oppressed by certain other groups historically. To what degree that's currently ongoing is a subject of debate and out of the scope of this book. But if victimhood is your primary emotional motivator, then you hate the oppressor, period. That much cannot be argued.

The next emotional state is fear. Some might say fear is the most powerful motivator, but that's not true. The most powerful motivator is actually love. It's only that it's *easier* to use fear as a manipulation tactic versus using love as a true motivator. Too many people are motivated by fear *because* it's the easiest tactic to weaponize to manipulate people. However, it's the lowest energy vibration to operate from, and its results are short-lived.

Moving up on the spectrum after fear is desire. When desire is your primary emotional motivator, it indicates that you are not satisfied with where you currently are in your life. To some degree, this is perfectly healthy, as we should all strive for growth and achievement. However, when it becomes your *primary* motivator, it brings with it a level of intrinsic unhappiness. Entrepreneur Naval Ravikant described it best when he said on X,

> **"Desire is a contract you make with yourself to be unhappy until you get what you want."**

Desire can also easily lead to greed.

The last emotional state in the physical realm on the fear spectrum is anger. I will skip the lengthy explanation here as we are all familiar with the negative effects of anger. Moving into the mental realm of the fear spectrum, there is entitlement, followed by pride. Entitlement is essentially the opposite of gratitude. If you've ever dealt with an entitled person, you know that an entitled person is one of the worst types to be around. I discussed pride at length in Chapter 1, so I will not belabor the point here.

Realms of Love and Fear

The next jump is quite an enormous one, however, because you are moving from fear into love. **In order to move from the fear-based states to the love-based states, the first step is courage.** It takes courage to move in love instead of fear. This means you have to be brave in order to move into love. This is because you're risking your emotions. When you move in love, you are risking the chance of being disappointed or hurt. As a result, many people use cynicism, pessimism, and negativity as a mask or a shield to prevent them from getting hurt. Ironically, they are still getting hurt; the only difference is that it's a gradual, self-inflicted pain rather than a sharp, acute pain from another person.

The truth is that most people aren't courageous. Most people aren't brave. Most people are actually cowards, and that's why they live in fear. It takes bravery to be optimistic, to have faith, and to believe in possibilities. Brave people don't let fear run their lives. Cowards do. They don't want the uncertainty and the risk that they could be let down from their hope and belief. So instead, they take the certainty of fear and negativity versus the uncertainty of love, hope, and possibilities. Fear runs their lives. These people are cowards, and cowards are *not* the kind of people who discover their diamonds.

Moving up after courage is reason, which makes sense. If you're brave enough to look at the possibilities and have some type of faith in a positive outcome, then you can look for the reasons why that might be the case. From a psychological perspective, reason serves as the framework through which we assess benefits, evaluate outcomes, and make pragmatic decisions about our personal, professional, and romantic relationships. Logic and reason are great, but they have their limits (see the discussion on paradoxes in Chapter 4 for more details).

Acceptance Is the Beginning of Spirituality

The vast majority of people stay in the physical and mental realm, meaning they are not spiritual people. Moving from the mental realm to the spiritual realm may be the biggest jump on the positive love spectrum. To enter the spiritual realm, you need acceptance. Acceptance means you are at peace with life, you are at peace with reality, you are at peace with the way you are, and you are at peace with the way the world is. Acceptance means you are not fighting reality (see Chapter 3 for a detailed discussion). Many people are at war with reality, and they cannot, and will not, ever win.

Most people never reach the state of acceptance as their primary emotional motivator. When you have true acceptance, it can eventually lead to inner peace, and it is the beginning of true spirituality. Another insight I have seen is that once you have a fundamental acceptance of what is, once you have a fundamental acceptance of reality, anxiety is no longer a major factor in your life.

Moving up from acceptance is wisdom, which is extremely powerful. Note that if you don't accept reality, you cannot ever have wisdom. There is a psychological definition of wisdom (see Chapter 6), but wisdom certainly has a spiritual dimension. From a religious perspective, all wisdom truly comes from God. Among other things, I believe wisdom includes the capability to distinguish what's truly important and the judgment to make good decisions while integrating vast and diverse perspectives.

Faith and Love

After wisdom, you have love and faith. Love is an extremely powerful motivator. The fact that endless amounts of art, music, and literature across diverse cultures over the centuries are all centered on love is a testament to how powerful true love really is. The thirteenth-century poet Rumi shared his insight that love is a natural state of being and that it's only self-imposed barriers that prevent you from experiencing love. By removing these barriers, you are not "finding" love but rather allowing it to emerge. Internal barriers that block the flow of love could include fears, past traumas, or insecurities. Journaling and therapy (see Chapter 9) and meditation (see Chapter 10) can help you uncover these barriers.

Faith is the other side of love. If you love someone, you have faith in that person. You have belief in that person. If you love your husband or your wife, you have faith in that person to do their best to serve you. Similarly, if he or she loves you, then they have faith in you to do the same. In 1 Corinthians 13:7, it says, "Love bears all things, believes all things, hopes all things, endures all things." So love and faith both have the enduring quality of hope.

Unconditional Love: A Divine Attribute

Finally, you have the highest level on the spectrum: unconditional love. Unconditional love denotes a selfless affection without any prerequisites or expectations, often seen as the epitome of pure love. In Christianity, it's epitomized by God's boundless love for humanity, often referenced by the Greek term *agape*. Within that unconditional love is grace, meaning giving people a second chance, and forgiveness. Grace and forgiveness are two of the highest values in that spiritual realm on the love spectrum. It's not a coincidence that the entire Gospel of Jesus Christ is a portrait of grace. It's a portrait of sacrifice. It's a portrait of forgiveness. Grace and forgiveness are really the highest, most elevated behaviors anyone can exhibit. If you've ever seen a story in which someone had a loved one murdered and they eventually forgave the killer, it's always very shocking and surprising. This is because grace and forgiveness are divine attributes and run counter to human nature.

You really have to be spiritual, if not also religious, to truly exhibit forgiveness and grace and unconditional love, because Jesus had all of those to a level that none of us can ever have. So that is the pinnacle, the peak of spirituality, and it points toward Jesus Christ. Unconditional love is God level, for lack of a better term. Jesus has unconditional love for all of us, and Christians try to be more like Christ because of this.

The Bible frequently tells the reader, "Do not fear" and "Do not be afraid." If you let it, fear can paralyze you and take away your power.

Don't Make Fear-Based Decisions

In a *Glamour* magazine article, Michelle Obama eloquently stated,

> **"Don't ever make decisions based on fear. Make decisions based on hope and possibility."**

This suggests that decisions driven by fear tend to be reactive and often hinder our personal and professional growth. Fear can cloud our judgment, block our creativity, and prevent us from growing and expanding. Decisions made out of fear rarely lead to long-term fulfillment. Usually, the best decisions that we make are the ones we choose in spite of fear.

Instead, it is better to base our decisions on hope. Hope represents optimism, a positive outlook on the future, and the belief that better things are possible. Decisions rooted in hope are more likely to align with our long-term goals and aspirations.

One of the issues holding many of us back from love-based decision-making is that we live in a fear-based society. The truth is that many organizations weaponize fear in order to manipulate us. The media is one example. Negative headlines or alarmist narratives get attention and can lead to more viewers or readers, which in turn lead to higher advertising revenue. Fear is also used to shape our decisions because it is a strong control mechanism. When people are in a state of fear, they might be more likely to give up control or make impulsive decisions. This tactic can be utilized by various entities to steer public opinion or behavior in a desired direction.

CHAPTER SUMMARY:

- Fear is the primary obstacle to listening to your inner voice.
- Letting go of fear and embracing love will help you reach your true potential.

- By consistently taking action despite fear, you move closer to discovering your diamond.
- Making decisions based on hope and possibilities pushes you out of your comfort zone, creating the pressure needed to form your diamond.
- If you've followed these steps consistently, you are ready for the final step: listening to your inner voice.

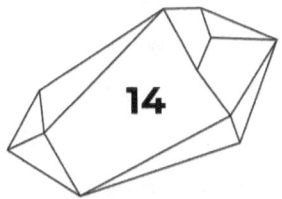

14

LISTENING TO YOUR INNER VOICE

"Cherish your visions and your dreams, as they are the children of your soul, and the blueprints of your ultimate achievements."

—NAPOLEON HILL

Steve Jobs had a vision. His inner voice told him that there could be a world where every person had a computer. During a time when computers were enormous, unwieldy machines only used by scientists and corporations, this vision was outrageous and seemed impossible to many. Yet his intuition, undeterred by societal norms, led to the birth of Apple Computer, Inc.[1] Steve Jobs's unyielding faith in his inner voice was the driving force behind his innovations. He sculpted a legacy marked by his unwavering belief in intuition, often in defiance of prevalent norms. His story is a testimonial to the synergistic potential of intuition and innovation.

His appreciation for the value of intuition began long before his Apple days, however. It was during a trip to India, immersed in a culture in which intuition was prized over intellect, that Jobs recognized the immense value of intuition. Reflecting on this period, he stated, "The people in the Indian countryside don't use their intellect like we do; they use their intuition instead, and their intuition is far more developed than in the rest of the world. Intuition is a very powerful thing, more powerful than intellect, in my opinion. That's had a big impact on my work."[2]

Another monumental moment came with the inception of the iPhone, of which his intuition was a major driver. The mobile industry was dominated by buttons and styluses, yet Jobs envisioned a device that was entirely touch-operated—a concept that reshaped communication globally. His team was skeptical, fearing the idea would flop, but Jobs's intuitive belief in the concept was unyielding. The result was a piece of technology that redefined communication, propelling Apple into a league of unprecedented success.

Jobs's knack for intuitive foresight wasn't just confined to products. In 1986, Jobs saw something unique in The Graphics Group, a division of Lucasfilm, and renamed it Pixar Animation Studios. Despite its financial woes, Jobs believed in its potential, his intuition sensing a pulse of innovation. Despite early financial struggles and spending $50 million, his intuitive belief in Pixar's potential led to a partnership with Disney, eventually culminating in the creation of the iconic film *Toy Story*.[3]

Investing in Pixar was a gamble that paid off remarkably: The company eventually merged with Disney, making Jobs Disney's largest individual shareholder.

His pursuit of intuitive design didn't stop there. The iPad, a tablet in a market dominated by PCs and laptops, was another testament to his belief in intuition over market trends. The iPad was met with skepticism, many failing to see the gap it filled in a market populated by laptops and smartphones. Jobs, however, sensed a need for a bridge device. He pursued this intuition with passion, leading to a device that carved out its own niche—further testament to Jobs's ability to sense market desires before they materialized.[4]

Jobs was known for his "reality distortion field" (RDF), a term coined by Bud Tribble at Apple Computer in 1981. This was an embodiment of Jobs's ability to convince himself and others to believe almost anything through a mix of charm, charisma, bravado, hyperbole, marketing, appeasement, and persistence. Tribble said, "The reality distortion field was a confounding mélange of a charismatic rhetorical style, indomitable will, and eagerness to bend any fact to fit the purpose at hand."[5] This RDF was Jobs's intuitive belief in the unseen, a belief that challenged reality to fit the vision his intuition whispered. Steve Jobs's legacy is a testament to the boundless potential that lies in heeding one's inner voice. His intuitive foresight, even in the face of skepticism, led to technological revolutions that shaped the modern world.

Finding Your Vision

We would all be wise to value our inner voice as much as Steve Jobs did. But you may be asking, "How can I do that? We all can't be Steve Jobs." The truth is that you can't listen to your own inner voice until you awaken to who you truly are. What's your vision? What do you constantly dream about?

You need courage to believe in your dream. You need to be brave to trust that your dream is achievable. You need faith in your intuition. Many people are limited by what seems to be possible. Those of us who discover our diamonds, however, know that there are no limits. You can't listen to any naysayers. If anyone says, "Be realistic" or "That's not realistic," then you need to limit your interaction with that person as much as possible. Whatever the achievement is, it always seems impossible until it's done. Dreams are very precious, and many people who have given up on their dreams will put their own limitations on you, and they often doubt your ability to realize your dream because they failed to turned their dreams into reality.

Self-exploration, critical thinking, and having an independent mind will lead you to asking yourself the right questions. As you follow this curiosity, you will be guided by your intuition or your inner voice, and it will lead you on the path to where you need to go. Your inner voice will gently speak to you; it will give you a nudge to go in a certain direction. To discover your diamond, you have to listen to the whispers of your inner voice. What have you always wanted to pursue, but you never had the time, the courage, or the permission?

One requirement to listening to your intuition is that you cannot be at war with yourself. The inner war must come to an end. There is no inner enemy. You must stop fighting yourself and be at peace to accomplish anything truly great in life. Success won't feel the same without inner peace and mental clarity. The most important victory is within your mind.

Those thoughts you are battling with aren't yours; they're other people's voices. We've all internalized voices from our childhood and early experiences, and it could be our parents, our teachers, ex-boyfriends or ex-girlfriends—it could even be from the media. Oftentimes these voices are critical, and they cause us to place false limits on ourselves. When you go into the wilderness (see Chapter 6), spending time in solitude to reflect will help you determine which thoughts are actually yours and which thoughts came from other people.

Find Your Diamond Dream

You may be wondering how you can determine when you've found the dream that will eventually lead you to your diamond. I don't have all the answers to that question, but I can certainly give some guidance based on my experience. The first thing to assess is the motivation for your vision. I can say with certainty that an ego-inspired fantasy is *not* a diamond-level dream. An example of an ego-inspired fantasy would be if you want to be a millionaire only so people can tell you that you're awesome. Or if you want to write a bestseller so people can pat you on the back and you can have the external validation of others' approval. Or if you want to make a certain amount of money so that the number in your bank account can finally tell you that you're enough.

In any of these cases, nobody's life is changing for the better because of it. Nobody will start a family because of it. Nobody will turn their life around because of it. Nobody will be inspired to do something productive with their life as a result of this vision. Any motivation that only gratifies your ego is *not* making the world a better place. Any motivation that is purely selfish and ego driven is *not* your diamond. It must benefit people outside of you. Your dream *must* be bigger than just you; any diamond-level dream must be in service of other people. Your diamond will always lead you to make the world a better place in some way, shape, or form.

If you're going to discover your diamond, you don't actually know where the path leads. You just have to have the faith that you are being led where you're supposed to be. You are being led where you are going to thrive. There is something very special inside of you, and only you can bring it to life. Once you are on the path and you are following your purpose, you will become unstoppable. Obstacles will still come, but you will navigate them much more easily.

Another thing to note is that your diamond will not just drop in your lap; you need to uncover it. You can only discover it by taking purposeful action every single day. The key is to follow your own intellectual curiosity. Listen to your gut feelings.

Think about what gets you excited. Think about what topics you always want to learn more about. What do you enjoy so much that whenever you do it, you lose track of time? Think about what you would still do even if you didn't get paid for it. Think about what you enjoyed doing as a child, but maybe you stopped doing it as you grew up.

Our intuition can be overshadowed by external influences or self-doubt. One of the main problems is that our educational system teaches us not to think for ourselves. We are taught *what* to think, not *how* to think. Blind obedience to authority is incentivized, and curiosity is not encouraged. We are rewarded for having all the answers, but not for asking the right questions. As a result of this, we must nurture our own curiosity, critical thinking, and individuality to eventually hear our inner voice.

Too often, we don't give ourselves permission to do the activities that bring us joy and meaning because we've been conditioned to believe that it's a waste of time. However, it's never a waste of time to pursue anything you're drawn to, because you're drawn to it for a reason. You might apply that knowledge in a way you could never have imagined. For example, my following my own intellectual curiosity is what led me to the research, life experiences, and perspectives that have inspired and informed my writing of this book. This happened completely organically, and I never anticipated it, and that's the beauty of it.

There is also a synchronicity and a convergence that happens when you listen to your inner voice. Eventually, when you are on the path to your diamond, you will start to hear the same ideas, concepts, or themes in different situations from different people. When something is being repeated to you across seemingly unconnected situations, usually it means it is a sign from God (or the universe if you are not religious), and you need to listen and follow it. On this path, your supporters will appear. The resources will be there. The opportunities will drop in your lap. When you answer the call of your inner voice, the details will take care of themselves.

Carl Jung stated in his book *Memories, Dreams, and Reflections*, "Your visions will become clear only when you can look into your own heart. Who looks outside, dreams; who looks inside, awakes." In other words, true clarity of vision is achieved only through introspection, by looking into your heart. You need to tune into your intuition to gain deeper understanding and clarity about your desires, values, and ultimate purpose. It's about moving from a state of external dependency to a state of internal empowerment. Everyone has dreams, but to turn those dreams into a reality, you must awaken.

Visions and dreams often originate from the subconscious mind, which is a reservoir of unprocessed emotions, experiences, and innate desires. They can be seen as the subconscious mind's way of communicating your deepest desires and potential pathways to fulfill your purpose. However, this requires conscious effort. It's about acknowledging, valuing, and reflecting upon the insights provided by your subconscious. This conscious engagement with your inner narrative is one of the ultimate steps toward discovering and uncovering your diamond.

CHAPTER SUMMARY

- Tuning into your intuition is essential for gaining deeper understanding and clarity about your desires, values, and ultimate purpose.

- By tapping into your inner voice and listening to your calling, you will eventually discover your diamond-level dream.

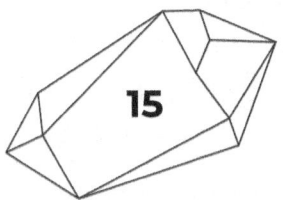

EPILOGUE: DISCOVER YOUR DIAMOND

> *"Your time is limited, so don't waste it living someone else's life. Don't be trapped by dogma—which is living with the results of other people's thinking. Don't let the noise of others' opinions drown out your own inner voice. And most important, have the courage to follow your heart and intuition."*
>
> —STEVE JOBS

On April 14, 2020, I began the process of drafting this book. We were a few weeks into a worldwide pandemic, and the entire world had shut down. This gave me an enormous amount of time to simply think and reflect. At this point in my life, I was aware that I had been through numerous challenges, situations in which others may have given up, and moments when I could have lost all hope and succumbed to despair and nihilism. But I never did. I kept the faith alive.

There were many mindset shifts and updates to my personal philosophy that I had to make to not only navigate these challenges successfully but also thrive because of them. On reflection, I realized that the entire story of my life was one of resilience, determination, and *anti-fragility*. For those who are unfamiliar with that last concept, Nassim Taleb popularized the concept of being anti-fragile, essentially meaning that what doesn't kill you makes you stronger.

I reflected on my life and realized that I was not only a much stronger, wiser, and more effective person because of the challenges I had been through but, most importantly, because of how I had dealt with those challenges, adapted to negative situations, and made the best out of seemingly hopelessly negative situations. It was through this reflection that I realized the power of the mind. And at this point, the desire to share my story with the world only grew.

On some level, I manifested this book. As I was going through various traumatic experiences and hitting rock bottom, I had so much faith that I would get through these challenges that, in the midst of one particular mental health challenge, I promised myself that I would share my story with the whole world. I visualized myself on a stage sharing my story of overcoming these challenges.

And on that cold day in April 2020, when the world had shut down, I believe this is what caused me to reflect on my life in a way that others could benefit from it. I began outlining the ideas that you see in Chapter 1. At first, I thought it might have

EPILOGUE: DISCOVER YOUR DIAMOND

been just a short talk, a speech, or a podcast episode since I had a podcast at the time, but the ideas and concepts kept growing and growing into the book you're currently reading. I'm including this here in this chapter to show you some of what went on in my mind as I was uncovering the diamond I found at my rock bottom.

Your process may not look anything like mine, but I am confident there will be similarities. Everything you have been through in your life is pointing you in a certain direction. All of your experiences, your pains, your hurts, your joys, your challenges, and your triumphs have a common through line, and it is only by reflecting on this that you will be able to find your diamond.

At a certain point, you will be so far down the path of self-discovery, spiritual awakening, and personal development that you will want to build something that will serve other people. Eventually, you will have transformed your life so much, you will want other people to realize what is possible for them. When you have lived through a transformation in your own life that you would have previously thought impossible, you will want to help others achieve the same. Knowledge is one of the few things that you continue to give away, but it multiplies instead of decreasing. Sharing insightful knowledge is similar to a flaming torch that can light many candles.

Your diamond will require you to create something and share it with the world. What good is a diamond if nobody can appreciate it? Matthew 5:15 says, "No one lights a lamp and puts it under a basket. Instead, a lamp is placed on a stand, where it gives light to everyone." When you have discovered your diamond, you will be compelled by a calling and a purpose in your life that is so crystal clear that you can physically feel it. You will have so much conviction in your decisions that others will wonder how you move with that level of certainty. When your life is organized in such a way that you are able to operate in your highest power, your energy level is different. You will also inspire other people around you to pursue their dreams and live in their purpose.

At this point, you are living a congruent life. You are in touch with your subconscious mind and your intuition. This congruency means that your thoughts, your words, and your actions all align. You no longer have the friction of cognitive dissonance that happens when you think something but don't speak it, or you speak something but don't act on it. You get the natural joy and fulfillment from confidently walking in your purpose. You are living in your "zone of genius," so you can speak from experience. Your interests and curiosities align with your current path. You've learned, read books, lived life, made mistakes, and grown. You've probably even hit a few life milestones.

Once you have found your inner voice, discovered yourself, and are following your dreams, you have found your diamond. Now you are free. At this point, your definition of success changes. You live by the quote: "What would you do if you knew you could not fail?" Since you have already let go of the illusion of failure (see Chapter 2), then you *know* you cannot fail if you are pursuing your purpose and discovering your diamond.

Chris Bumstead, bodybuilder and five-time Mr. Olympia winner as of the time of this writing, encapsulates this idea perfectly in a post on Instagram:

> **"When your success no longer becomes attached to an outcome, the only way you can lose is if you quit on yourself."**

If you have discovered your diamond, then you are *not* a quitter; therefore, you *cannot* fail. Failure is not a true obstacle; it is an artificial construct that you need to transcend. Chris's insight was that you have to detach yourself from the outcome of your work. In this way, you revise your definition of success so that it is not dependent on any outcome. In order to redefine success in this way, you have to do the work for something bigger than yourself. True success comes from pursuing a purpose that is true to who you are. Therefore, the only true loss is giving up on your path.

Once you are at this point, you realize that the journey *is* the destination. You never "arrive," because the goal is continuous learning and growth. You always remain open to learning by always remaining curious, helping to avoid complacency.

One way to confirm that you've found your diamond is to examine the concept of *ikigai*, a Japanese philosophy that translates to "a reason for being." Ikigai is found at the intersection of what you love, what you are good at, what the world needs, and what you can be paid for (see the Venn diagram in Figure 15.1). It's a balanced combination of passion, mission, vocation, and profession, guiding people toward fulfillment and societal contribution.

15.1 *Ikigai*

When you find your diamond, you've discovered a purpose that resonates deeply with your soul and benefits the world around you. True fulfillment comes not from external achievements but from aligning your actions with what you love, what you excel at, and, importantly, what serves the greater good. When you feel that your purpose encapsulates your passions, leverages your strengths, meets the world's needs, and has the potential to sustain you, you can be confident that you have indeed found your diamond.

As you harness this alignment—the synergy of your passions, strengths, societal contributions, and economic sustainability—you embark on a lifelong journey of self-discovery and service. This path, illuminated by the diamond you have unearthed at your rock bottom, is neither straightforward nor static. It is a dynamic voyage that continuously evolves as you grow and as the world changes around you. Each step on this journey offers new opportunities to deepen your understanding of yourself and to expand your impact on the world.

Remember, the essence of this journey lies not in reaching a final destination but in the growth and happiness that come from living in harmony with your deepest values. Embrace each day with the joy and curiosity of a perpetual learner. Stay committed to your path, and let your diamond guide you through the challenges and successes that life invariably presents.

With each challenge faced and each lesson learned, you will find that your capacity for impact grows and your sense of fulfillment deepens. This is the true measure of success—a never-ending advancement toward personal excellence and collective well-being. Keep shining brightly like the diamond you are, and let your journey inspire others to find their own paths to fulfillment and success.

NOTES

Chapter 1

1. Holiday, R. (2014). *The Obstacle Is the Way: The Timeless Art of Turning Trials into Triumph.* 19–23. Portfolio/Penguin.
2. Tedeschi, R., & Calhoun, L. (2004). Posttraumatic Growth: Conceptual Foundations and Empirical Evidence. *Psychological Inquiry: An International Journal for the Advancement of Psychological Theory, 15*(1), 1–18. https://doi.org/10.1207/s15327965pli1501_01
3. Kessler, R., Sonnega, A., Bromet, E., Hughes, M., & Nelson, C. (1995). Posttraumatic Stress Disorder in the National Comorbidity Survey. *Archives of General Psychiatry, 52*(12), 1048–1060. https://doi.org/10.1001/archpsyc.1995.03950240066012
4. Kaufman, S. (2020, April 20). Post-Traumatic Growth: Finding Meaning and Creativity in Adversity. Scientific American Blog Network. https://blogs.scientificameric rowth.
5. Tedeschi, R. G., Shakespeare-Finch, J., Taku, K., & Calhoun, L. G. (2018). *Posttraumatic Growth: Theory, Research, and Applications.* Routledge.

Chapter 2

1. Moran, J. M., et al. (2014). Spontaneous Mentalizing Predicts the Fundamental Attribution Error. *Journal of Cognitive Neuroscience, 26*(3), 569–576. https://doi.org/10.1162/jocn_a_00513

2. Dweck, C. (2008). *Mindset: The New Psychology of Success*. Ballantine Books.
3. Goel, S. (2020, July 11). *Domino's Is Not a Pizza Delivery Company. What Is It Then?* The Strategy Story. https://thestrategystory.com/2020/07/11/dominos-digital-transformation/

Chapter 3

1. Quinn, S. (2021, September 15). *Dennis Schroder Pokes Fun at His Decision to Pass on $84 Million Lakers Contract on Instagram*. CBSsports.com. https://www.cbssports.com/nba/news/dennis-schroder-pokes-fun-at-his-decision-to-pass-on-84-million-lakers-contract-on-instagram/
2. Suzuki, S. (2011). *Zen Mind, Beginner's Mind: Informal Talks on Zen Meditation and Practice*. Shambhala.
3. Farnam Street. (2019, August 27). *Ray Dalio: Open-Mindedness and the Power of Not Knowing*. Farnam Street Blog. Retrieved July 7, 2024, from https://fs.blog/ray-dalio-not-knowing/

Chapter 4

1. Murphy, J. (2013). *The Power of Your Subconscious Mind*. Wildside Press.
2. Jung, C. G. (1969). *Psychology and Alchemy: Collected Works of C.G. Jung* (2nd ed., Vol. 4,). Princeton University Press, 18.
3. Jung, C. G. (1967). *Alchemical Studies: Collected Works of C.G. Jung* (Vol. 13). Princeton University Press.

Chapter 5

1. Open Sky Wilderness Therapy. *Areas of Impact*. Retrieved May 15, 2022, from https://www.openskywilderness.com/areas-of-impact/

2. Brown, B. (2010). *The Gifts of Imperfection: Let Go of Who You Think You're Supposed to Be and Embrace Who You Are.* Hazelden.

3. Brown, B. (2019). *Braving the Wilderness: The Quest for True Belonging and the Courage to Stand Alone.* Random House, 32.

4. Grover, T., & Wenk, S. L. (2014). *Relentless: From Good to Great to Unstoppable.* Simon & Schuster, 78.

5. Kramer, D. (2000). Wisdom as a Classical Source of Human Strength: Conceptualization and Empirical Inquiry. *Journal of Social and Clinical Psychology, 19*(1), 83–101. https://psycnet.apa.org/doi/10.1521/jscp.2000.19.1.83

Chapter 6

1. Krumrei-Mancuso, E., & Rouse, S. (2016). The Development and Validation of the Comprehensive Intellectual Humility Scale. *Journal of Personal Assessment, 98*(2), 209–221. https://doi.org/10.1080/00223891.2015.1068174

2. Esser, J., & Lindoerfer, J. Groupthink and the Space Shuttle Challenger Accident: Toward a Quantitative Case Analysis. *Journal of Behavioral Decision Making, 2*(3),167–177. https://doi.org/10.1002/bdm.3960020304

Chapter 7

1. Schrum, H. (2023, May 3). *Bud Light's Missteps in the Dylan Mulvaney Controversy: A Lesson in Failed Brand Strategy and the Importance of Authenticity.* LinkedIn. https://www.linkedin.com/pulse/bud-lights-missteps-dylan-mulvaney-controversy-lesson-hogan-shrum/

2. Mcleod, S. (2018, updated 2023, October 24). *What Is Cognitive Dissonance Theory?* Simply Psychology. www.simplypsychology.org/cognitive-dissonance.html

3. Manson, M. (2023, April 23). Vulnerability: The Key to Better Relationships. *Mark Manson.* https://markmanson.net/vulnerability-in-relationships

4. Holiday, R. (2019). *Stillness Is the Key.* Portfolio.

5. Kaufman, S. (2021). *Transcend: The New Science of Self-Actualization.* Penguin Books.

Chapter 8

1. Rosmarin, D. H. (2021, June 15). *Psychiatry Needs to Get Right with God. Scientific American.* https://www.scientificamerican.com/article/psychiatry-needs-to-get-right-with-god/

2. Resilience. *Psychology Today.* Accessed May 23, 2024, from https://www.psychologytoday.com/us/basics/resilience

3. For example, see Khosla, M. (2017). Resilience and Health: Implications for Interventions and Policy Making. *Psychological Studies, 62,* 233–240.

4. Schiraldi, G. (2017, November 17). What Do Resilient People Look Like? *New Harbinger Publications.* https://www.newharbinger.com/blog/self-help/what-do-resilient-people-look-like/

5. Brenan, M. (2020, December 7). *Americans' Mental Health Ratings Sink to New Low.* Gallup. https://news.gallup.com/poll/327311/americans-mental-health-ratings-sink-new-low.aspx

6. Rosmarin, D., Bigda-Peyton, J., Kertz, S., et al. (2019). A Test of Faith in God and Treatment: The Relationship of Belief in God to Psychiatric Treatment Outcomes. *Journal of Affective Disorders, 146*(3), 441–446.

7. Todd, M. [@iammiketodd]. (2023, April 15). *Faith begins where understanding ends— if you knew it all or could figure it out, it wouldn't be faith* [Video]. TikTok. https://www.tiktok.com/@iammiketodd/video/7222288879536147758

8. Chopra, D. [@DeepakChopra]. (2014, January 7). *Religion is belief in someone else's experience. Spirituality is having your own experience.* [Post]. X. Accessed May 23, 2024, from https://x.com/Deepak Chopra/status/424339573783539712

Chapter 9

1. Moore, A. (2021, March 16). *How to Design a Life That Eliminates Distraction and Enables Hyper-Focus.* Medium. https://anthony-moore.medium.com/how-to-design-a-lifestyle-that-eliminates-distraction-and-enables-hyper-focus-cde3b613b1ff

2. Wood, W., & Rünger, D. (2016). Psychology of Habit. *Annual Review of Psychology, 67*, 289–314. https://doi.org/10.1146/annurev-psych-122414-033417

3. Anderson, J., Baird, P., Davis, R. Jr., et al. (2009) Health Benefits of Dietary Fiber. *Nutrition Reviews,* 67(4), 188–205.

4. Merriam-Webster. (s.v.) Calorie. In Merriam-Webster.com dictionary. Accessed April 17, 2024, from https://www.merriam-webster.com/dictionary/calorie

5. Stumborg, M., Blasius, T., Full, S., & Hughes, C. *Goodhart's Law.* CNA. Accessed May 23, 2024, from https://www.cna.org/reports/2022/09/goodharts-law

Chapter 10

1. Kaufman, S. (2021). *Transcend: The New Science of Self Actualization.* Penguin Books.

2. Scipioni, J. (2021, December 18). *Billionaire Ray Dalio Credits His Success to 40 Minutes of Meditation per Day—Here's How He Does It.* CNBC. https://www.cnbc.com/2021/12/18/billionaire-ray-dalio-how-transcendental-meditation-helps-me-succeed.html

3. Jackson, P., & Delehanty, H. (2014). *Eleven Rings: The Soul of Success*. Penguin Press, 51–52.

4. Terpstra, D. *Interview with Joe Dispenza—You Are the Placebo, Making Your Mind Matter*. Soul Love. Accessed May 23, 2024, from https://www.soullove.com/interview-with-joe-dispenza-you-are-the-placebo/

5. Lazar, S. W., Kerr, C. E., Wasserman, R. H., Gray, J. R., Greve, D. N., Treadway, M. T., McGarvey, M., Quinn, B. T., Dusek, J. A., Benson, H., Rauch, S. L., Moore, C. I., & Fischl, B. (2005). Meditation Experience Is Associated with Increased Cortical Thickness. *NeuroReport, 16*(17), 1893–1897. https://doi.org/10.1097/01.wnr.0000186598.66243.19

6. Taren, A. A., Creswell, J. D., & Gianaros, P. J., (2013). Dispositional Mindfulness Co-Varies with Smaller Amygdala and Caudate Volumes in Community Adults. *PLoS One, 8*(5). https://www.ncbi.nlm.nih.gov/pubmed/23717632

7. Hölzel, B. K., Carmody, J., Vangel, M., Congleton, C., Yerramsetti, S. M., Gard, T., & Lazar, S. W. (2011). Mindfulness Practice Leads to Increases in Regional Brain Gray Matter Density. *Psychiatry Research: Neuroimaging, 191*(1), 36–43. https://doi.org/10.1016/j.pscychresns.2010.08.006

8. Gerritsen, R., & Band, G. (2018, October 9). Breath of Life: The Respiratory Vagal Stimulation Model of Contemplative Activity. *Frontiers in Human Neuroscience, 12*. https://doi.org/10.3389/fnhum.2018.00397

Chapter 11

1. Beck, L. (2024, March 7). *Warren Buffett's Key to Success: "Say No to Almost Everything."* Yahoo Finance. https://finance.yahoo.com/news/warren-buffett-key-success-no-161048764.html?guccounter=1

NOTES

Chapter 12

1. MacMullan, J. (2020, April 5) *Jordan, Russell, Kareem, Even the King of Pop—the Astonishing Mentors Who Shaped Kobe Bryant.* ESPN. Accessed September 19, 2023, from https://www.espn.com/nba/story/_/id/15193525/jordan-russell-kareem-even-king-pop-astonishing-mentors-shaped-kobe-bryant (Subsequent quotes are taken from the same article.)

2. Ferrazzi K., & Raz, T. (2014). *Never Eat Alone: And Other Secrets to Success, One Relationship at a Time.* Currency.

Chapter 14

1. Isaacson, W. (2011). *Steve Jobs.* Simon and Schuster.

2. Medeiros, J. (2018). *Here's Why Steve Jobs Said Intuition Is Absolutely More Powerful Than Intellect.* Goalcast. https://www.goalcast.com/steve-jobs-said-intuition-is-more-powerful-than-intellect/

3. Broussard, M. (2016, November 23). *History Between Steve Jobs and Pixar Highlighted in New Book 'To Pixar and Beyond.'* MacRumors. https://www.macrumors.com/2016/11/23/steve-jobs-to-pixar-and-beyond/

4. Isaacson, W. (2011). *Steve Jobs.* Simon and Schuster.

5. Golis, C. (2018, June 26). *Emotional Intelligence and the Reality Distortion Field.* Emotional Intelligence. https://www.emotionalintelligencecourse.com/emotional-intelligence-and-the-reality-distortion-field/

For certain sections of this book, I used generative AI to brainstorm ideas and create initial drafts.

www.ingramcontent.com/pod-product-compliance
Lightning Source LLC
Chambersburg PA
CBHW030443090526
44586CB00044B/588